# Intuition Workout

A Practical Guide
to Discovering and Developing
Your Inner Knowing

*by*
*Nancy Rosanoff*

Published by

Aslan Publishing
310 Blue Ridge Dr
Boulder Creek, CA 95006
USA

Rosanoff, Nancy, 1949-
Intuition Workout.

1. Intuition (Psychology)–Problems, exercises, etc.
2. Intuition (Psychology) I. Title.
BF311.R644 1988     153.4'4'076     88-19437
ISBN 0-944031-13-7 (pbk.)

© 1988, Nancy Rosanoff

Cover design by Diane Naugle and Charles Waltmire
Illustrations by Ira Harmon
Book Production by Brenda Plowman
Printed by Specialty Web
10 9 8 7 6 5 4 3 2 1

# Acknowledgements

First of all, I would like to thank all of my students, past present and future, for having the courage to explore unknown territory with me and for making this book possible. Sandy Freeman, wherever you are, thank you for inspiring me in this career direction. The New York Open Center and Esalen Institute in Big Sur, California deserve thanks in this department also giving my teaching such a wide audience. I would also like to acknowledge Aslan Publishing and Dawson Church in particular for seeing the value of my work and taking the time to work with me on the creation of it. Thanks to Brenda Plowman, also from Aslan, for coordinating the production of this book and thanks to Ira Harmon for his illustrations. Thanks to Steve Nichols for taking my photograph. I would also like to acknowledge my Macintosh Plus for making the writing of this book so enjoyable. Mac, you have inspired me to write many more.

I would like to thank Ray Cicetti, Kathy Bateman, John Nonna, Daniel Korin, Linda Hall, David S. Burr, Ann Depta, Charles Simpkinson, Gail Greenstein, Nancy and Jack Goldstein, Edgar Mitchell, Angela Manno, Judith Stanton, Pat Rodegast, Penny Rice, Roy Rowan, Jack Himmelstein and Tom Mullen for reading the manuscript and giving me such great advise. Thanks to Betsy Westendorf for inspiration on the "Body Intuition" exercise, Stewart Emery for inspiration on the "Traffic Light" exercise, and Marilee Zdenek of The Right Brain Experience, who inspired the "Releasing Fears" exercise. Also, I would like to thank Kathy Bateman again for spending so much time encouraging me and believing in me, for helping out with the kids and for being my friend. I would like to thank Janet Dubin for keeping things going in my office with such a cheery attitude before, during and after the writing of this book.

Finally, I would like to acknowledge and thank my family, beginning with my husband, John Krysko, for being the first person to recognize the value of what I was trying to do and for his continued support through the years; my parents, Peg and Tom Dorr, for their never-ending love and acceptance; my sisters, Julee, Andrea, Kathy, Aimee and Janice, for being my friends; and last, but not certainly not least, I would like to thank my children, Tamar Ragir and Jessie Krysko, for their love and support.

# Contents

# List of Main Exercises

# Introduction

My husband and I had just moved out of an urban environment in an attempt to lead a simple, "homesteader" life in the mountains of northern California. We lived four miles down a dirt road, with no plumbing or electricity, for two years. When we first arrived, we were quite inexperienced in country living, and everything was a new experience.

Our dog had also been a city dog. She was not accustomed to the life of a country dog. She loved to run off through the woods, and would eventually return.

One day she did not return. Some neighbors from about a mile away came over to visit us. They told us that our dog had just killed 20 of their ducks, which they raised for food. They had our dog tied up, and wanted us to come over and shoot her, because dogs of her species – she was a coon hound – are natural hunters. The chances were slim that she could be trained not to hunt, and to stop killing livestock.

We had just moved in and did not want to start a feud with our neighbors, so we went over to where our dog was tied up and prepared to shoot her. They had a gun, and wanted us to do it right away. I couldn't believe what I was doing. I actually had a gun pointed at the head of my dog and I was about to pull the trigger.

I started to cry, and I begged the neighbors to give us two weeks to try and retrain her. If she still hunted livestock after that, I would shoot her. They agreed, but had

1

little hope that it could be done.

For the next week and a half we tried everything everybody told us about how to train a dog not to hunt. We starved her, beat her and tied a dead duck around her neck. Nothing worked; our time was running out.

One day I took a long walk. I sat down in a meadow and cried. There must be a way to train her! Suddenly a little voice in my head said, "Get a bell." I thought, "Well, I'll give it a try."

It worked. When she had the bell on, the ducks and chickens would hear her coming and run away. She soon lost interest in chasing animals. We then acquired some chicks of our own so that she would really learn not to chase them, and we never had a problem with her hunting animals after that. Our neighbors were amazed and pleased. Since then, I have not made a major decision or even many minor ones without consulting my Intuition first.

That was an event that convinced me of the validity of the intuitive mind. Now, you may be thinking, "It's logical to think of putting a bell around the dog's neck." But this never occurred to me, or to anyone else in the situation. No one I spoke to during that time had ever mentioned a bell as a form of training. The message clearly came from something inside of me that I was not consciously aware of and could not consciously contact at that point.

Since then, I have made a study of Intuition, and have created an exercise program to train it and strengthen it. This book is a compilation of what I have discovered.

These methods have been used by thousands of people from all walks of life in my seminars: housewives, executives, advertising people, scholars, financial planners, job applicants – anyone who faces choices and challenges in the course of a day – and who doesn't?

Your Intuition is a resource, an additional level of information that is tremendously useful when sorting out all the options. Plus, you don't have to wait for a crisis for Intuition to strike. It can be a reliable, accessible tool. Once trained, Intuition can be a resource you can draw upon any time; it will be a trustworthy advisor and friend. The following pages contain the "how-to's" of consistently using this resource in your life.

Intuition, and the exercises on the following pages, are not meant to be a substitute for professional advice and counselling. However, your Intuition, once trained and available to you, is useful as an additional layer of advice and information about situations you may be facing. But it is not meant to be used in place of thinking for yourself, being responsible, and gathering all the relevant information which affects your circumstance before making decisions. If your situation requires the advice of a doctor, attorney, accountant or other qualified professional, make sure you get it.

CHAPTER

# 1

## Intuition Warm-up

### Intuition Bodybuilding

Intuition is like a muscle. It needs exercise to become strong, flexible and reliable. Many of us have intuitive flashes, such as a sense of who is on the phone before we pick it up, or a feeling that we knew something was going to happen before it happened. These flashes are just a brief flexing of an ability that we all have, but which few develop.

This book is designed to help you develop a training program for your Intuition which will build it into a source of insight reliable enough for you to call upon when you need it.

Because you have decided to read this book, I can assume that you already know that Intuition is an important resource, but you may think that you have to wait for a flash of Intuition; that it is not something you can consciously control. In this book I will show you that this preconception is not true. Intuition can be there for you when you ask for it. Intuition can be there for you when you need it most.

Before we go any further, let's back up a bit and start with a working definition of Intuition. The most useful and general definition that I use is: **Intuition is when we know, but we don't know how we know.** Going a little deeper, it is an inner knowing, or knowledge that comes from within.

This inner knowing may be stimulated by something or someone external to us, but the information bubbles up from inside. We know it is from within because it is usually accompanied by a strong physical, visual and/or emotional sensation. Each person will have a slightly different experience of this sensation, but there are some similarities, which we will be discussing throughout the book.

## How To Use This Book

Each chapter of this book corresponds to a weekly training program. Each discusses a particular aspect of Intuition, provides a main exercise for you to practice during the week, and gives different thoughts or variations on the main exercise to be practiced daily. Each chapter includes examples and personal stories of people who have used these exercises. Common questions that apply to the topic are discussed.

I strongly suggest that you read the whole book through once. Then go back and do the weekly program. Some readers will find they need more than a week to complete the weekly program. You may find that it takes you two or three weeks to get to all the exercises. This is perfectly all right.

Others may go through more than one chapter each week. This is perfectly alright too. It is important that you find your own speed and stick to it. If, at the end of one particular week, you feel that you have not been able to apply the exercises for that week to your life even once, repeat them for one more week. If, after that extra week, you still feel that you have not incorporated the material, go on. You can go back to whatever chapters you want to after completing the entire program. I also strongly recommend that you keep a journal while doing the training program outlined in this book. Your journal will show your progress, your weak points, and give you feedback on the results of your intuitive work. I prompt you during each exercise to remind you to make an entry, although anytime you want to write in your journal is fine.

## Types of Intuition

Intuition communicates in a unique way with each person. Intuition Workout provides the exercises which will help you determine how your Intuition will speak to you. It will be up to you to practice that method until you are confident with it.

There are three primary ways in which Intuition speaks to us: **through images and symbols, through feelings and emotions, and through physical sensations.** Because Intuition is not necessarily verbal or logical, we need to become sensitive to the more subtle language of symbols, feelings and physical sensations in order to hear what it wants to tell us.

There are three types of Intuition: mental, emotional and kinesthetic (or physical).

**Mental** intuitives experience Intuition as something close to *thought*. It is a more masculine, goal-oriented form of Intuition which I have seen people in financial and business careers use. It is like a thought that you did not ask for, or a thought that is persistent. Mental intuitives often feel as though they are making something up when their Intuition speaks to them.

**Emotional** intuitives *feel* their Intuition. It is the traditional "woman's Intuition," a vague or specific feeling that cannot be explained, but is usually right. One may just feel bad about something, or good about something.

Emotional intuitives may feel a mild form of depression when Intuition indicates that something is not right. They will know whether someone is happy or sad just by walking into a room with them, or by hearing them say "hello" on the phone. They may feel the same feeling themselves, without realizing that they are picking up thoughts and feelings from someone else. Emotional intuitives will use the words "like" and "I don't like." They decide based on how they feel.

**Kinesthetic** intuitives have *physical sensations* that communicate information. They may have a gut feeling, or something that excites their heart, or something that gives them a pain in the neck: these are all forms of kinesthetic Intuition. Kinesthetic intuitives will feel "comfortable" or "uncomfortable" about something.

Most often people have a combination of the above three, though one form may be dominant. Rarely is someone totally one type. We categorize them only to indicate that there is more than one way to perceive intuitive information.

All three types of people can perceive Intuition through visual, feeling or sensing modes, although usually the mental intuitives are visual and sensing; the emotional intuitives are visual, feeling and sensing, and the kinesthetic intuitives use feeling and sensing.

## Intuitive Information:

Unformed urge
experienced as:

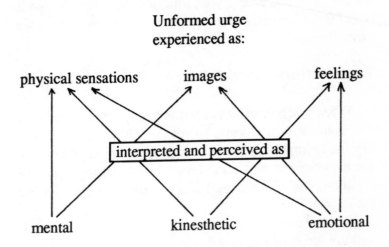

All these forms of Intuition need to be trained and developed in order to be reliable. I will say it now, and will say it many times in this book: **it is important to study the difference between a valid Intuition and a fear or a desire.** Weeks three and four are devoted to understanding your own fears and desires and how they distort your Intuition.

## How to Use the Intuition Warm-Up

The first warm-up exercise is designed to help you determine what type of Intuition you have. It is called a visualization exercise, although the name is a little misleading. I will be giving you images to follow, but some people will will "feel" things rather than "see" anything.

Some will neither "see" nor "feel," but will "think"; it

will be a little like *pretending* that you are following what I am saying. All these ways are fine. They are just indications of how you access your Intuition. So, even though it is called a visualization exercise, go with your own experience.

## Preparations for the Warm-Up

When you are ready to try this or any other exercise in this book, it is important to set the right mood. This is especially important in the beginning. Later on, when you are experienced and confident when listening for your Intuition, you will not need such an elaborate mood to set the stage.

But for now, take a few moments to make sure you will not be disturbed by other people, phone calls or door bells. Make sure you have a comfortable chair or couch. I also recommend that you sit to do the exercises, rather than lying down. Later on, a prone position may work well, but in the beginning, lying down puts most people to sleep.

Some people like to play relaxing, soothing, meditative or background music; others find any music distracting. Suit yourself. The most important ingredient ensuring the success of the exercise is your attitude. The fact that you bought this book is a great beginning. It means that you intend to develop a relationship with your Intuition.

Keep an open attitude. Anything is possible, and anything can happen. You do not need to analyze during the exercise; you can do that later. You do not need to think about the exercise while it is happening. Just observe.

You may want to share the exercise with a friend, and take turns reading it to each other. You can also read the exercise into a tape recorder and play it back to yourself. If you have the <u>Intuition Workout</u> tape, you can use that.

If you record it or read it to someone, be sure to read slowly and clearly, pausing a few moments at the commas, with longer pauses at the periods and even longer pauses between paragraphs, in order to give yourself and your friend time to let the images form. You will need about a half hour of quiet time to do this exercise. When I guide classes through this exercise I play meditative music as background music to help create a mood of relaxation.

When you are ready, sit down in a comfortable chair, take a few deep breaths, close your eyes and be attentive to what may happen.

\* \* \* \* \*

## Intuition Warm-up

*Imagine yourself walking down a street. Any street. Notice what kind of day it is, and what time of year it is. See and experience as many details as possible about the street, and the day, and what is going on around you. How are you feeling as you walk down the street? Hear the traffic; notice what is happening all around you.*

*As you are walking, become aware that there is a grocery store or produce market a few blocks in front of you. Guide yourself toward the store. Find yourself in front of the store and look at it. Notice any details about the store.*

*Now walk into the store and go to the produce department. When you get to the produce department, walk over to the citrus fruit section. When you get to the citrus section, pick up an orange. Feel it, notice its weight; see it, notice the color. Touch the skin and feel the texture.*

11

*Begin to peel the orange and notice the texture of the inside of the orange peel. Now you can even smell the fragrance of the orange. Keep peeling until the orange is completely peeled.*

*Now pull off a section of the orange and lift it to your mouth. Take a bite of the orange and chew it. Taste it. Feel the juice going down your throat as you swallow it. Are you enjoying this? Eat as much of the orange as you would like to.*

*When you are finished with the orange, go over to the lemons. Pick one up and hold it. Feel its weight. See the color of the lemon. Notice the texture of the skin. Find a knife and cut off a slice of the lemon. Now you can smell the fragrance of the lemon. Bring the slice up to your mouth. Now, take a bite and feel what the lemon does to your mouth.*

*Put the lemon down and walk out of the store. Once you are back on the street take a look around. Has anything changed? Notice the sounds, sights, smells. Walk back up the street the way you came. Notice again the day, the season, the weather. Slowly bring yourself back into your chair and take a few deep breaths. When you are ready you can open your eyes.*

\* \* \* \* \*

## Impressions

Take a few moments to write down what happened to you. Include any unusual events or things that happened that I did not say anything about. Notice particularly whether you saw images, felt the experience, or thought it. It is certainly possible that a combination of any or all of these modes is what happened to you.

What can you learn from this exercise?

For some it is a very emotional experience. The road they walk down is something out of their past – their childhood or a favorite home. It may be nostalgic. This person is probably an emotional or perhaps kinesthetic intuitive.

For others it is a combination of pretending and sensing. Perhaps they imagined a produce market on a street where none exists. Perhaps they noticed that no one said anything when they walked out of the store without paying. These are signs of a mental intuitive.

Some of my students have become very involved with what to do with the juice from the orange, and how to get it off their fingers; others drop the peelings on the floor, something in real life they would never do.

These are all creative solutions to problems in the exercise. All of the elements of this situation have probably occurred before, though not in this very order. Your mind might recall the sticky juice, and re-present that problem for you to play out. Your creative problem-solving ability will get a little exercise in the process!

13

# CHAPTER

# 2

## -WEEK ONE-
## Meet Your Intuition

*How do I know the ways*
*of all things at the beginning?*
*By what is within me.*

—Lao-Tsu

## Your Relationship With Your Intuition

Our first step must be to establish a relationship with
our Intuition. This involves finding the location of your
Intuition. If you are kinesthetic, you will *feel* where your
Intuition is. If you are mental, it will probably seem like
you are making it all up, or it may seem like a combination
of past experiences brought together. If you are a "feeling"
type, the exercise will feel real, or like an important dream.
And of course, you may well have some combination of
all three experiences.

## Don't Try

The important factor for everybody is to NOT TRY. Trying means that you are making an effort, and pushing or forcing the images or feelings. Trying also implies that you do not really think that this will work on its own, so you had better consciously and rationally **make** something happen.

Remember that Intuition is non-rational and non-linear. Our normal thinking modes will not be able to contact Intuition. You are aiming at linking with a more subtle way of thinking and feeling, so let go and let something different happen.

If nothing happens, THAT'S OK! Go ahead and do some of the other exercises. It's better to have nothing happen than to force something to happen.

To do this exercise fully, please give yourself at least half an hour of undisturbed time. You may want to put on some soft, meditative music or play a pre-recorded tape of this exercise back to yourself. If you have the tape of <u>Intuition Workout</u> you may use that. Sit comfortably, and be sure to breathe before and during this exercise.

* * * * *

### MAINTENANCE EXERCISE:
### MEET YOUR INTUITION

*Take a few full breaths. Feel that every breath is taking in relaxation. With every outbreath, you exhale all your tensions, distractions, thoughts.*

*Begin to imagine an ideal place for yourself. A place*

where you can be creative, peaceful, and just be yourself. A place designed just for you. Whatever and wherever you would like it to be.

Take your time and let the most ideal place emerge in your imagination. See or sense as many details about this

*place as possible: the furniture, the colors, the surround-ings, and the equipment, tools and toys you would like to have there. Let it all emerge in your mind.*

*Let it emerge so strongly that you feel yourself there. What does it feel like to be in this place? What does it feel like to be in the place that is designed for you, for your comfort, for your creativity, and for your serenity? If there are windows, look out to see where you are located. If you are outdoors, look around at the surrounding environment. What is the view from here? Is it an important aspect of this creative workroom?*

*Somewhere in this room or environment, there is a series of five barometers. Let yourself find them now, and go to them. Each barometer indicates how a part of you is doing. The barometers have a scale from one to ten, with one being low, and ten being very high.*

*The first barometer indicates your physical well-being. You do not project what you feel onto the barometer. Let the liquid in the barometer indicate to you the state of your physical well-being, without your trying. Just accept what it indicates to you.*

*The next barometer indicates your emotional well-being. Watch while the liquid in the barometer rises and stops at the number which best exemplifies your emotional well-being.*

*The next barometer indicates your mental clarity. Let this barometer indicate to you the state of your mental clarity.*

*The fourth barometer indicates your spiritual well-being. Perhaps you have not thought of this part of your being for a while. Just let the liquid in the barometer rise, and indicate the state of your spiritual well-being, whatever that may mean to you.*

*Finally, the fifth barometer indicates your overall well-being. Watch as the barometer lets you know your overall state.*

*Step back and spend a few moments reflecting on what the barometers have told you.*

*Now, find a comfortable place to sit or lie down in this wonderful place. Make yourself comfortable. Look around and notice more details about your place.*

*Take a deep breath and invite in your Intuition. Let go of any preconceived thoughts and let your Intuition come into your place and visit you.*

*It may take any of a million forms. Perhaps your Intuition comes in as an animal, as a person, as a spirit, or perhaps it is a presence: something you cannot see, but you know is there. Take a few moments to let this happen.*

*When you know that your Intuition is in this place with you, say "Hello." Find some way to communicate with your Intuition. It may not speak, but it may move, or send telepathic messages to you. Ask your Intuition if it has anything it would like to communicate to you right now.*

*Spend a few moments listening to what your Intuition is communicating. It may be by a feeling that you experience, or it may be by something your Intuition indicates to you by words or movements. Whatever it is, accept it and remember it.*

*Now, thank your Intuition for coming to you, and say good-bye for now.*

*Go over to where the barometers are and take a look at how you are doing now. Remember that the first barometer is your physical well-being; the second, your emotional; the third is your mental clarity; the fourth is your spiritual well-being, and the final barometer is your overall state.*

19

*It is now time to leave your wonderful place and to come back to where you are sitting. Take a few deep breaths and let the image and the feeling of this place fade away. Take your time, and when you are ready, open your eyes.*

Take a few moments to write down your impressions.

\* \* \* \* \*

## Common Experiences

This exercise, Meet Your Intuition, constitutes the Maintenance Exercise for the first week of your Intuition Workout. There are many, many reactions students have had to this exercise, and I will share with you the common themes that recur.

The question I hear most often after this exercise is, "How do I know that my impressions are real, or valid? It seems to me that I am just making it up as I go along."

The answer to that question, of course, is that you *are* making it up. Where do these impressions come from if not from you? It is *your* imagination, *your* mind, *your* Intuition that is following this exercise. Just because you feel that you are making it happen does not mean that the impressions are not valid. **They are valid for you because they came from you.**

There is a subtle difference in experiencing these impressions that is important to understand. Sometimes the impressions begin with the feeling that "I am putting this here and making it up" – and then the impressions take on a life of their own. The impressions or images take unexpected turns or do something that was not planned or conceived by you first. This is probably the most common way that people begin to open to their Intuition.

Sometimes people begin the exercises by feeling that the impressions are coming to them from some source other than their conscious mind. This experience is quite valid and indicates an Intuition that is already in communication with the conscious mind. It indicates that Intuition is accepted as a valid form of thinking. It has been given its particular place, or mode, separate from logical thinking, but connected to it.

In other people, all the impressions feel like they are planned and coordinated by the conscious mind. This is a good way to begin to establish communication with your Intuition. The major key to working with your Intuition will be your ability to let go, stop trying, stop analyzing, and trust the impressions you receive.

## Silly Intuition?

Another reaction to this exercise is to *not* feel comfortable with your Intuition. One student of mine had an animated mushroom come into the room as her Intuition.

Her first reaction was, "How silly! What kind of Intuition do I have?" It turned out that her Intuition came in the form of humor most of the time, and when she became too serious, her Intuition didn't work. So the symbol for her Intuition, the animated mushroom, became a friend she could trust to give her advice that would lighten her up.

## Scary Intuition?

Someone else had a scary image for their Intuition. It was a frightening figure in a black cloak. At first the

21

student backed off and wanted out of this exercise, but I advised him to go back and talk to the cloaked figure. After a brief conversation, the cloak came off and the figure became a strong leader-figure.

It became clear that the student was frightened of his own Intuition, and felt that following it would lead to self-destruction. After confronting that fear, his Intuition showed its true nature as a leader, which was really what the student was afraid of: his own leadership skills that would emerge as he began to trust his Intuition, and follow its advice.

We all have fears of what will happen if we do things that are not accepted by the people close to us in our lives. No one wants to feel rejected and unaccepted by others, and we usually feel that listening to our Intuition is going to tell us something that will set us apart from others and isolate us. This fear usually has no basis in reality. Chapter Three is all about fear. If your fears get in your way all week, skip to that chapter before returning to Chapter One.

## Reunion

Some people experience a profound feeling of coming back to something very valuable that they had not realized they had missed. Meeting Intuition with this feeling is like meeting an old friend.

This sometimes occurs to people who had a strong connection with Intuition as a child or young person, and then, for any number of reasons, stopped listening to their Intuition.

Re-establishing a relationship with Intuition may open up doors to feelings we had many years ago. The exercise itself may be full of memories of childhood, and other times of your life. This means nothing, other than that you once had a relationship with your Intuition – and the rest of the book may go much easier for you as you become reacquainted.

For other people the exercise will feel like meeting a new friend, and may be accompanied by tingling sensations, sometimes tears, and a feeling that something new is opening inside you. That feeling indicates that a connection is being made with your Intuition. It is a natural and full experience that many, many people share with you.

## Frustration and Rebellion

Sometimes students become uncomfortable following the design of the exercise as described. There is no need to let this frustrate you. There is no need to feel that you have to force yourself to follow the instructions as they appear. You can change things around, ask questions that occur to you, and direct the exercise in whatever way you feel is most beneficial to you.

The following excerpt is from the journal of a student who had this type of experience. She solved a situation that was unique to her.

"I remembered what the first two barometers, physical and emotional, measured. But I had to go back in the instructions to see what the other three had been – so much for my mental clarity!

"I felt like I should get the barometers out of my room before lying on the couch again. I didn't want them in my room. If I had known we were going to use them again later, I think I could have concentrated on the next part of the exercise better.

"Every barometer had improved since the first time.

"My Intuition removed the barometers for me when I wanted that. My Intuition is a beautiful Angel figure that never speaks. She has wings and often cradles me in them. What bliss! She is clearly a part of myself; the part that comforts and nurtures."

In the beginning it may be difficult to determine which approach works best for you, but in time, and by using a tape recording of the exercise, it becomes easier. If you are listening to a tape, you don't have to think about what comes next. You can listen to the tape, and then do what is most comfortable for you, knowing that the next instruction will be there when you need it.

Enjoy this exercise and repeat it as many times as you would like. Below, I have listed several complementary and extended versions of this exercise for you to practice during the week. After doing the first exercise at least two times on day one and/or day two, do at least one of the following exercises each day from day three to day seven.

* * * * *

## DAILY EXERCISES:
## ASK YOUR INTUITION A QUESTION

**DAY ONE AND TWO:** Go through the Meet Your Intuition exercise.

**DAY THREE:** Before you begin your exercises, think of a problem, decision, or situation in your life which would benefit from some advice from your Intuition. Write it down in your journal. Then, when you do the Maintenance Exercise above, present the situation as a question to your Intuition. Give your Intuition the time and opportunity to answer you. Remember that the answer may not be verbal. Your Intuition may show you the answer through actions, a feeling, or perhaps through a telepathic communication.

**DAY FOUR:** When you meet your Intuition this time, see if you can feel or touch your Intuition. Even if you first met your Intuition as a vague feeling, or presence, now see what your Intuition would feel like if you could touch it or him or her. Remember the feeling throughout the day, and this will bring you in closer contact with your Intuition.

**DAY FIVE:** Today when you go into your special place to meet your Intuition, play a game together. Throw a ball to it, and let it throw the ball back to you. Even if your Intuition is just a presence, or filmy creature, it can still play catch. Your Intuition is creative and clever and will find a way to catch and throw the ball.

**DAY SIX:** Today when you meet your Intuition, ask it to sit or stand over your shoulder all day. If your Intuition is large, it can shrink for this exercise, and if your Intuition is shy, it can come forward today. If your Intuition is a presence, that presence can be on your shoulder today. Throughout the day, remember that your Intuition is there, and talk to it. Ask it how you are doing while you are involved in a task, a meeting, a project; driving or traveling or whatever. Also, listen carefully, because, during the day, your Intuition will speak to you when you haven't even talked to it, or asked it for advice.

**DAY SEVEN:** When you meet your Intuition today, tell it about something in your life that is bothering you. It may be a personal situation, a co-worker or friend who is disturbing you, a project you have not been able to complete, anything in your life right now that is distracting you. Let your Intuition comment on this to you. Listen to what your Intuition has to say, or communicate. Remember that Intuition may communicate using feelings, sensations, words or movements. Write all the results and experiences in your journal.

* * * * *

## This Week's Results

By now you will have the beginnings of a good working relationship with your Intuition. You know how to contact it, him or her. It, he or she knows how to contact you. And, by the way, it was my own Intuition that helped me come up with all these exercises!

You may have been able to listen to the advice your Intuition offered you and seen its value. Or perhaps you heard clearly what your Intuition told you, yet still hesitated to follow through on the advice. That's OK. Just keep trying and listening. Your Intuition is not going to go away. Take some time to explore what it is you are afraid of and realize that you *always* have a choice. Your Intuition is just one part of you. You can consult it and then make your decision.

*You* are the one in charge of your life. Intuition just happens to be a good source of information and advice that we can contact when we need to. It's like listening to your lawyer, your accountant, or your friend. You may agree with some of the things they say, but that does not mean that you are going to do it all their way. You still have to make up your own mind and do what is comfortable for you.

CHAPTER

# 3

## -WEEK TWO-
## Listening To Your Intuition

*My first bid, hastily made, was $165,000. Then somehow that didn't feel right to me. Another figure kept coming, $180,000. It satisfied me. It seemed fair. It felt right. I changed my bid to the larger figure on that hunch. When they were opened, the closest bid to mine was $179,800. I got the Stevens Corporation by a narrow margin of $200. Eventually the assets returned me $2 million.*
*—Conrad Hilton*

This week's workout is one of my personal favorites. I like it because after this week, you will have tangible results and evidence that your Intuition is real and is communicating with you.

This week will also feel like a break from last week's intense push. Last week you had to break through your initial skepticism. This week you can begin to make your relationship with your Intuition personal. There are only three exercises for this week. Spend a day with each one,

and then use the one of your choice once a day for the remainder of the week.

These exercises are designed to tune your Intuition for specific situations. You may find that one exercise works wonderfully for you while the others do not seem to suit you. That is perfectly acceptable and I encourage you to use the exercises that are comfortable and successful for you. Later on, a few weeks down the road, you may want to go back and try the ones that did not work so well the first few times. Keep notes in your journal on your progress.

* * * * *

## EXERCISE ONE:
## DECISION PATHS

For this exercise you will need to think of a decision you have to make and list the alternatives you are considering. It is best to consider no more than four alternatives at a time until you become comfortable with this exercise. Write your specific decision and/or situation in your journal and number the alternatives. You are now ready to begin whenever you have about 10-15 minutes of quiet time.

*Sit down, close your eyes and make yourself comfortable. Take a few deep breaths. Let go of the thoughts and distractions of the day.*

*Imagine yourself walking down a path. Any path. Take a few moments to notice the scenery. What season is it? How is the weather? What time of day is it? Are you enjoying this walk?*

29

*While you are walking, go over the decision or situation that you are currently considering. List and number your alternatives in your mind. And continue walking and enjoying the scenery.*

*As you are walking, up a short way ahead of you, the path breaks up into several paths. The main path splits into as many paths as you have alternatives to your decision. When you come to the place in the path where the road splits, stop.*

*Each path represents one of your alternatives. Number the paths in any direction that is comfortable to you, and let those numbers correspond to the numbers of your alternatives.*

*Take your time, and take a deep breath. Let it out slowly. Slowly travel down one of the paths.*

*Notice how you feel.*

*Where does the path take you?*

*How comfortable are you on this path?*

*Does this path feel right?*

*Take as long as you want to explore this path.*

*When you have finished, go back to the place where the paths meet. Choose another path, and explore it as you did the first one. Continue exploring until you have experienced each path.*

*When you are finished, take another deep breath and let it out slowly.*

*When you are ready, you can open your eyes, and record the events of this exercise in your journal .*

**ADVANCED EXERCISE:** *Add a path with no clear choice, an unknown, which represents a choice which has not emerged to you as yet.*

\* \* \* \* \*

## Interpreting the Results

This exercise has become automatic for me and for many of my students. I can do this exercise in about three minutes. Any decision I have to make first goes to my Intuition. I create a path for the choice, and move down it. How does it feel? Does it feel right? Is it uncomfortable? If it is at all uncomfortable, I do not choose that decision.

Sometimes I know right away that something is wrong for me and I can say no. At other times, it is unclear. The feeling is neither a distinct yes or no. In that case I do nothing. I do not make the decision, because it is not time to make it. Right Intuition really depends on right timing. If we jump for something before it's time, we may miss an opportunity, or create more problems than we need to deal with.

## Examples

Recognizing the rightness of the paths is a personal feeling. For example, one of my students used this exercise when making a career decision. One path she walked down was a straight, wide highway. Another one was a rocky, uphill mountain climb.

She knew that the uphill path was the right one for her because she knew she needed a challenge. She did not want the easy path; she wanted the challenge that was going to lead her to the top, even though she knew, especially after this exercise, that it was not going to be easy.

Another student chose the path that was straight, because it felt right to him. For him it was time to do something that was easy, instead of always making it hard on himself.

31

One student interpreted the uphill path as follows:

"I am in a lush forest with beautiful greenery on both sides of my path. My path branches into three very different environments. The first path is a steady incline of solid rock. This path does not seem treacherous but is almost boring: step after step, like climbing an endless staircase.

"The second path is a continuation of the primary path, but it becomes very wide. I can see the greenery on either side but it's very far off. It is extremely dry and dusty. I don't feel lonely but mentally I know I must be.

"The third path is virtually impassable. There are gnarled vines and twisted trees blocking the path.

"I feel very much as though I am making the paths correspond to my alternatives. My decision was whether to go into a business partnership with someone. Path #1 means, 'Don't go in to the partnership.' Path #2 means, 'Go into it in a limited way,' and path #3 is, 'Go into it entirely.'

"I added a path: 'Do the business alone.'

"For this alternative, my path looked like a steep mountain climb. I get hot and tired, but I feel rejuvenated when I reach the top, like the lift that comes from doing any physical exercise."

These images open the door for us to understand how we feel about a situation. For each of us, the decisions we make are based on what is going to work for us, not what would work for someone else. It is still up to individuals to make decisions for themselves. Before we make any decision, we should consult our Intuition, as well as other information available to us.

\* \* \* \* \*

## EXERCISE TWO:
## SENSING BODY INTUITION

For this exercise you will need another problem, situation, or decision about which you would benefit from some advice from your Intuition. Describe the situation as simply as possible in your journal. This exercise is written in a step by step manner. Read through all the steps first and then go back and follow the procedure.

1. *Think of a problem or situation that would benefit from the advice of your Intuition.*
2. *Close your eyes and go from thinking about this situation to feeling it. In other words, if you could feel this situation, where in your body would you feel it? You may feel it in more than one place. If so, focus on where you felt it first, or most strongly.*
3. *Spend a few moments focusing on what the sensation feels like.*
4. *If this feeling could speak to you, what would it say?*
5. *What would this feeling like you to know about your situation?*
6. *What action could you take that would relieve this feeling?*
7. *Thank your Intuition.*

\* \* \* \* \*

Write down all the information you received from your Intuition in your journal.

This exercise will help you tune in to the intuitive information stored in your body. As I stated in the

Introduction, one way that Intuition speaks to you is through physical sensations and feelings, and this exercise is a key to unlock that source for you.

If you are a kinesthetic intuitive, this exercise will probably be one of your favorites. You will feel actual physical sensations. If you are an emotional or mental intuitive, this exercise can also work for you, but a little differently than for the kinesthetics.

The emotional intuitives will experience emotions which are centered in certain places in the body. Mental intuitives will think through this exercise and will pretend where in their bodies they may feel this situation.

## The Value of Practice

At first this exercise may feel uncomfortable and silly to you, but please keep trying it. After a while you will become so attuned to what your body Intuition is telling you that you won't even have to ask, or stop to do this exercise. You will automatically know how you *intuitively* feel about something. In the next chapter we will consider the difference between *emotional* feelings and *intuitive* feelings.

## Examples

Have you ever felt uncomfortable about something that was going to happen, for no apparent reason at all? Perhaps later on, during the event or situation, you found out what you were uncomfortable about.

For example, one time my husband wanted us to go to a particular store together. I felt uncomfortable about going. It just did not feel right. But I ignored the feeling because usually doing something like that would be fun. It turned out that the store was closed for some special occasion that we did not think about. No real big deal, but I was reminded that my Intuition is always something to listen to, and at least find out more information about what it's telling me before proceeding.

One person felt an unusual sensation in her fingers. Her question was about what to do next in her life, since her children were grown and she had more free time available. The tingling in her fingers communicated to her that she might want to try working with clay sculpture. She had never considered this before, although she had always been good with her hands. She gave it a try. It turned out to to be very valuable new outlet for her creative expression.

How did she get from tingling fingers to clay sculpture? That is part of the magic of Intuition.The thought or clay sculpture came from inside of her. It is not a logical connection. Tingling fingers could mean something different for someone else. In her case, the tingling fingers were simply what was required to bring her intuitive knowing to her conscious mind.

In some cases I have seen students make erroneous interpretations of what their intuitive trigger indicates. For example, this woman might have tried clay sculpture and been disappointed. Perhaps she was really being asked to write an article that would release her creative energy.

The important thing to remember and write down in your journal is *your initial feeling,* image or sensation, *without any analysis* – just a description of what happened. Then you can write an analysis. In this way you can later go back and determine whether your subsequent analysis indeed matched the meaning of the original impression.

Another student was planning a two week overseas vacation. A couple of weeks before she and her family were to leave, she began to feel very uncomfortable about travelling on the plane. She was in touch enough with her Intuition enough to know that something was going to happen, but she also knew intuitively that she had to wait until her feelings became clearer, or she heard more clearly.

In this uncomfortable limbo, she had a tremendous amount of nervous energy. The week before they were to leave, she used this energy to pack, clean the house, and take care of overdue paperwork.

The afternoon before the day of their flight, she received a call from the airport. Their flight had been cancelled, and they would have to take the midnight flight that night if they wanted to go. They had to be at the airport two hours in advance, and it took an hour and a half to get there, provided there was no traffic.

Because she was so thoroughly prepared, packed and ready to go, the family made it to the airport easily.

In this case there was no clear analysis, just an uncomfortable feeling. The appropriate action took place out of the uncomfortable feeling. Understanding did not take place until the event actually occurred, quite a while later.

## From the Known to the Unknown

Getting back to the exercise, the most difficult part of this exercise for most people is getting to step two. Moving from thinking about something to feeling it in our bodies is not what we normally do, so it will take a little more time to let it happen. At first it may seem like you are imagining the feeling. That is perfectly OK.

In a way, you are imagining it, so start from there and proceed. If you feel like you are making it up, go along with the exercise anyway, and regard it as an experiment. If you are "making it up," this will become apparent later, while if it is indeed Intuition, you will find that out later too. For now, just do the exercise and worry about the results later.

## Don't Jump To Conclusions

Part of our mind wants to jump to conclusions. This undermines the value of our Intuition. If you consider it, deciding that intuitive information is not valid before testing it is very unscientific. It will never do to come to conclusions before you explore the territory. So give yourself a chance; notice how you are judging the information, and continue to do the exercise anyway. Record your results – and wait and see!

One student felt his kinesthetic sensation in his head, as a throbbing headache. He had to make a decision about whether to accept a new management position that was being offered to him, or stay in his current job as a copywriter.

His headache communicated to him that he really enjoyed his present, creative job. Moving to management would mean a dramatic change in his duties. He liked the idea of a raise in salary, but was uncomfortable with the management part of the deal. His Intuition was telling him that having to oversee other people and their work was not going to be enjoyable for him.

The action he could take to relieve his headache was to talk to his boss and find out if there was a way he could get a raise, perhaps take on more projects, without having to manage anyone else. It worked.

Again, the physical sensation brought the intuitive information to his conscious mind.

## Bodies Are Smart

Our bodies hold alot of information. Every feeling, thought and impulse, no matter how vague or subtle, gets registered in our neuro-muscular structure. The body does not need words or thoughts to do this, so even if our conscious minds are not aware of what we are registering or what we are feeling about something, the body is. This exercise helps us access intuitive information by taking the time to become sensitive to what the body has registered about a specific situation.

* * * * *

### EXERCISE THREE:
### PREPARING FOR FUTURE EVENTS

This exercise is designed to be used with an upcoming important event in your life, perhaps an important meeting, party, get-together, interview, presentation or performance.

If there is no important future event coming up, you can practice this exercise with little future events, ones that are not so crucial. Before you begin this exercise, go over what you know about this event already: when it is supposed to take place, who else will be present, where it might happen, etc. Write all this information in your journal.

While you are doing this exercise, the following hints may be helpful:

**Be open to general sensations.** Since we are talking about the future, people will get general sensations, though a few will get specific details. Focus on the major feelings, moods and experiences. Details such as how the room looks, what someone is wearing, etc., will probably be irrelevant.

**Keep focused on what you want to accomplish.** What is important here is what happens to you, how you feel about it, and how you need to accomplish it. Stay aware of your attitude during the event, and watch yourself.

*Sit down and make yourself comfortable. Be sure you have about 20 minutes of uninterrupted time. Close your eyes and take a few deep breaths, exhaling fully. When you are alert, fully present and relaxed, go into the environment where you first met your Intuition.*

*Take a few moments to make yourself comfortable there. Notice if anything has changed about this place, and notice if there is anything you would like to change about it. Do whatever you need to do to make yourself content here.*

*One item that you need to have in this environment is a full length mirror. You can put it anywhere, even away in a closet, if you do not want it ito nterrupt the space. But know where it is, and how to get to it. Another thing you need to have here is a door or opening that leads to some other place, other than the way you entered into this environment. Notice, now, where that opening or door is.*

*As you walk toward the new opening or door, know that on the other side of it is the future event you are preparing for.*

*When you get to the door or entry way, stop. Take a deep breath. Let it all out. Now, open the door and walk into the future event.*

*Spend as much time here as you would like to, observing and experiencing. Ask yourself, "Who is here, what is happening, will this be right for me?"*

*When you are finished, go back into your main room or environment. Go over to the full-length mirror. Know now that this is not an ordinary mirror. This mirror has the ability to reflect your Intuitive knowing back to you.*

*Ask the mirror how you could improve the event, using the information you just acquired. Listen to what the mirror reflects back to you. You may hear the information in words, or sense the feelings in your body. Perhaps you will know telepathically what the mirror wants to communicate to you.*

*Leave the environment, take a few moments to bring yourself back to where you are sitting. Breathe. Open your eyes, and write down all the information you received.*

* * * * *

## Understanding Your Results

The first time most people do this exercise, they may experience a vague sense of what might be happening, or some fuzzy feelings about the situation. Students also get confused about whether they are seeing what they want to see, or what they are afraid will happen. If you experience any of these sensations, write your results in your journal, and wait for the event.

The best way to evaluate Intuition is to record your experiences and compare them with what happens. You may be surprised at how accurate your Intuition was, or how some images or feelings that you did not understand during the exercise make more sense after the event. This is normal, and after doing the exercise for a period of time, your understanding of what your Intuition is communicating will increase.

## Examples

Even the first time it is used, this exercise has produced some amazing results for some of my students. One student told of her experience in <u>Savvy</u> Magazine. At the time she worked for an advertising magazine and was looking for another job. She had an upcoming interview, for which she used the above exercise.

During the exercise, while she was in the future event, she experienced the interview proceeding rather badly. While in her potential boss's office, they were interrupted several times by phone calls and visitors. She felt as though she and her potential boss just were not able to make contact. She left the Future Event feeling discouraged.

Then she went over to the mirror, as you did, and the mirror explained to her how to improve the situation. The mirror suggested that she invite her interviewer out to lunch, that she wear a certain suit, and that she ask for an amount of money greater than she had been considering previously. She followed the advice of her Intuition. She got the job at the salary she asked for.

Another student of mine, a hospital administrator, was preparing her department for an audit at the time of our class. She was directing her staff to go back into old files and become familiar with past data. She used the upcoming audit for this exercise. While she was in the future event, she experienced the auditors asking for current, mostly obvious information concerning what was going on now in her department.

She realized that if she kept going back into the past for her preparation, she would not be prepared for the simple, obvious questions. She redirected her staff, and, of course, the auditors did exactly as her Intuition predicted.

Both these ladies' Intuition spoke to them quite clearly and directly. Yours may not be so clear. Most of the time, for beginners, the information from this exercise takes the form of vague feelings or sensations, or perhaps some images. Please do not be discouraged. The best approach is to write down what happened and sit on it for a few days. Go back to your notes and see if it triggers anything. The information will become clear in time.

## Common Sense or Intuition?

Are the above examples cases of "common sense" or actually Intuition? The solutions to these problems sound like common sense, but they had nevertheless not come to either lady's mind. Sometimes consulting Intuition brings us back to obvious things that we had been complicating unnecessarily. If so, that in itself is a valuable service.

Perhaps, a skeptic might say, just taking a little time out to reflect guided those experiences. But even if working with Intuition simply encourages us to take the time we need to reflect, it is valuable.

There are many, many more stories, including my own, but now it is your turn to try it. This exercise can be the most difficult of the three for this week. In my experience, it is because a lot of us feel we do not have the right to know what is going to happen.

## Cheating?

Some of us feel it is cheating to be so prepared. But in my experience, most successful people prepare for what may or may not happen. Whether you have a sense of Intuition speaking, or simply form a habit of preparing for everything, a key to success is anticipating what someone is going to ask or want or do, and be prepared.

Listening to our Intuition is a skill we can develop and

it is as important a skill as learning to organize our time or our thoughts. We have had ample opportunities to learn to organize our thoughts. Now it is time to give ourselves the opportunity to develop our Intuitive skills.

After you have done each of these exercises once, repeat the ones you feel most comfortable with during the week. Be sure to record your results, because it may be a week or so until your future event happens. When it does, you will want to go back to your notes and compare.

CHAPTER

# 4

## -WEEK THREE-
## Trusting Your Intuition
## Understanding Your Fears

*The only thing to fear is fear.*
*— Franklin D. Rooseveldt*

Now that you have experienced some of the joys and benefits of listening to your Intuition, we can go on to deal with the major obstacle that keeps you from trusting your Intuition: FEAR.

We all experience fear in many aspects of our lives. Fear seems to be a part of being human. This is not a detailed report on fear, just on the effect fear has on Intuition in my experience and that of my students.

## Stop Fear From Stopping You

Our goal is not to abolish fear, but to defuse it. Fear should not stop you from doing what is important for you to do. It should never stop you listening to your Intuition.

I am not talking about fear as in knowing that something is dangerous, and deciding not to do it. That is smart! I am talking about fears that constantly get in your way.

## Fear Gets In the Way of Success

For instance, you may know that it is time for you to receive a raise in salary, but because you are afraid to ask for it, you do not.

That fear can be seen as a fear of your Intuition. You know inside of you that it is time to ask. Perhaps there are circumstances around you that support your Intuition, such as: others with your background have received raises; you have been working for a certain number of months, etc. But still you do not trust yourself enough to go ahead and ask for it. You are afraid something will go wrong. So you hold yourself back and end up very unhappy.

This kind of fear creates a barrier to listening to your Intuition. When we encourage fears by giving in to them, we give them strength and automatically these fears appear whenever we want to do something a little differently from what we are used to. We all have fears such as this, and sometimes need to push ourselves a little to try something, even though we are afraid to break what I call the Fear Barrier. Remember that courage is *not the absence* of fear. Courage is the ability to act – even when you **are** afraid. It takes courage to break through the Fear Barrier.

## Fear Blocks Intuition

Another kind of fear that gets in the way of Intuition is a persistent fear about the same thing. Examples of this kind of fear include someone who is always afraid of flying, or someone who is always afraid of swimming, or driving on highways, etc.

These kinds of fears can be visualized as constant walls in our mind that keeps Intuition from working in that one particular fear area. If you are always afraid of flying, you will never know when your Intuition is telling you not to fly and when flying is OK. You have an automatic response of "No, it is not safe." That automatic response is quite strong, and Intuition, especially during the developmental stage, is not strong enough to get through. This is an extreme example of something that we all experience on a minor level.

A common example that appears in almost all my classes is a fear of communicating feelings to another. The fear is, "If I say what I really feel, they will reject me, or not like me anymore, and I'll never get what I want." This fear keeps people from listening to their Intuition when it tells them to ask for something, get something off their chest, or to say "no" to something that someone wants them to do.

Breaking through this kind of fear requires a psychological understanding of ourselves and our behavior, and a willingness to understand our fears and not let them interfere with what is important to us.

Some fears come from our cultural training and background. To let go of these fears does not mean throwing away the values and memories of our families. It does mean that we do not want them to interfere with our ability to listen to our Intuition.

Sometimes fears come from an experience that happened a long time ago and has been forgotten. But the fear remains, and still affects us today.

If severe fears or phobias persist, you may need professional help in understanding them. This book is not intended to deal with debilitating and phobic fears. They require a deeper understanding of ourselves to deal with.

## How Intuition Gives Warnings of Danger

Some of you may be asking yourselves, "But aren't there some things to be afraid of? And won't our Intuition want to warn us about things that may be dangerous to us? If we ignore our fears, isn't that naive and dangerous?" Good question! Yes, our Intuition wants to guide us away from danger, but *it does not do so with fear*.

Intuition is neutral. We may hear the message that today is not the day to go to the grocery store, but when we hear it it will be neutral. It will not have a strong fear element or strong emotional content. We may react afterwards with nervousness, fear or excitement. But the first feeling is neutral. By neutral I mean just that: the message is a statement of fact, or a feeling of fact.

## Know Yourself

We are getting into an aspect of Intuition in which our knowledge of ourselves becomes very useful. For instance, I know that I am a "doer." I'm more comfortable with doing than with waiting. Sometimes I just do not get around to doing something which I know intellectually I should. I have learned by experience to trust these sensings and not take action until it is "right." But if I were someone who always waited until the last minute, or habitually put things off, I couldn't trust those sensings. If that were the case, I might then need to learn to act promptly.

A woman in one of my classes had her first experience

of this the other day. All week she practiced doing only what felt right and nothing else. A friend had called her and left a message wanting some information. She did not call him back right away, as she would always normally do. Although she felt uncomfortable not calling him right away, whe wanted to wait until it "felt right." When it finally did, it turned out to be the best time for this person to receive the call. She was amazed.

Self knowledge helps us see these subtle differences. In her case, she had to distinguish between her uncomfortable feeling that stemmed from her personality pattern of always taking care of things immediately, and her intuitive feeling for when to call. The urge to call did not come accompanied by any big fanfare – just an impulse to pick up the phone and dial. Intuitive information is neutral.

## Premonitions

A strong example is someone who has had a premonitory dream about someone they love who dies. In the dream we know for a fact that something has happened: our grandmother is dead. *Then* we react emotionally, and feel the loss of someone dear to us, but the initial sensation was of fact.

This is a strong example, but I know that many people have had a similar experience. Before we develop our Intuition consciously, and it wants to communicate with us, it can usually only get through our conscious thoughts with a strong, important event. Once we develop and listen to our Intuition, it will cover a wide range of topics that are not so intrusive and scary.

I have had many students who have had dreams or premonitions such as the one above. On this basis they decided that developing their Intuition would be too frightening. They did not want to develop a skill they associated with strong feelings about people they loved. Yet at the same time, they had no control over their impressions.

With the exercises in this book, they developed a control over their Intuition, and a broader range of topics their Intuition communicated on. Eventually, the strong, dramatic impressions did not occur as a large proportion of their intuitive input.

\* \* \* \* \*

## CORE EXERCISE
## FOR THE WEEK:

For this exercise, it is best to start with a current situation, or a recurring situation that causes anxiety. This exercise is designed to help you examine something that causes fear or hesitation. So think of something, get something in your mind, that makes you feel afraid or anxious. Choose one in which you would like to stop letting your fear control you. Begin by writing a brief description of your fear in your journal.This exercise will need about 30-40 minutes of uninterrupted time. It is also helpful to play soft, non-interfering music in the background.

## RELEASING FEARS

*Make yourself comfortable. Take a few deep breaths. Close your eyes. As you breathe, imagine that you are breathing in sparkling, luminous energy that enters into you with the air you are inhaling.*

*This luminous energy goes into your body and breaks*

up any tensions, dissolves any distractions, and releases
the thoughts of the day. As you exhale, feel the tensions,
distractions, and thoughts leaving your system. Continue
breathing in this sparkling energy and releasing tension for
a few moments.

   Imagine yourself walking on a beach; feel the sand
underneath your feet; feel the sun above you. Let the
warmth of the sun relax you. Let go. Enjoy the beauty surrounding you. Listen to the sound of waves. Perhaps there
are some birds flying around. Smell the smells of the
beach. Take your time and feel yourself there. Enjoy the
calm beauty of the ocean.

   Walk over to a blanket that is lying on the beach
waiting for you. Sit on it; make yourself comfortable. Gaze

51

*out at the ocean and watch the rhythm of the waves. Begin to think of something that causes you fear or anxiety. Perhaps it's related to a troublesome problem that's currently in your life. Perhaps it's something more general. Whatever it is, let it come into your awareness.*

*As you think about it, stay in your body, and feel what part of your body this problem is most closely related to. When you think of this problem, fear or anxiety, where do you feel it? Sense its location in your system. Let it form into a tangible, physical feeling within you. With your mind, go to that part of your body. Sense it; feel what that tension or anxiety feels like. Is it sharp or dull? If it seems to be in several parts of your body at the same time, go to where it begins, where it starts, and follow it as it moves throughout your body.*

*Now reach into your body and remove it. Pull it out. Hold it in your hand. Now you can look at it. What does it look like? Does it have any color? Does it have any texture? What does it feel like as you hold it in your hand?*

*Begin now to talk to this thing in your hand. Ask it what purpose it has ever served for you. Ask it when it began. When did you first begin to feel this tension, this anxiety? Why is it still with you? Is it still serving a useful purpose?*

*Now, with your other hand, separate out anything that is still useful about this thing that you pulled from your body. Separate out into your other hand what it still valuable, so that now in one hand you have the part of this thing that is still useful and in the other hand you have what is no longer useful. Feel their different weights. Feel their different textures. Notice the difference between your two hands.*

*Now take what is still useful and put it back into your*

body. *You may want to put it back where you removed the whole thing or you may feel it necessary to put it someplace else. Whatever seems right to you is okay. Soak this useful energy into your system. Breathe into it. Let it energize you and revive you. Feel with your whole being why it is useful to you, why you need it.*

*Now dig a deep hole in the sand and bury what is in your other hand, what is no longer useful for you. Bury it deep and as you cover it over with sand, know that it is now being dissolved. It is being neutralized by the sand and the water so that it can no longer hurt you or cause you tension.*

*Make sure the sand covers over it completely, so there is no trace of where you buried it. It is completely out of your sight, completely out of your feeling. It is now completely gone. It has dissolved out of your system.What you have left is what is very useful to you, what gives you energy.*

*Notice how you feel now that this problem, this tension or anxiety or fear, is gone. Let yourself feel how differentl you feel now that this is no longer in you. Stand up and walk down the beach, sensing again how different you feel without that tension or fear holding you back. Soak in the sun. Enjoy the sounds of the waves and the birds. Release any residual tension or fear, letting it completely out of your system.*

*Now bring yourself back to your current reality, feeling free from this anxiety, this fear. And when you're ready, open your eyes and take some time to write down what happened. Enjoy the rest of your day. Let your Intuition remain with you.*

\* \* \* \* \*

This exercise really speaks for itself. In order to recognize what fears are hindering us, we need to pull them out of us and look at them squarely. Only then can their hold on our inner knowing be released.

## Examples

Many powerful experiences have resulted from this exercise. One I remember distinctly was conveyed to me by a woman who asked about a situation involving her daughter. The fear was a stiff pain located through both of her shoulders and her neck. When she removed it, it looked like a strip of metal that was holding her shoulders in place.

When she asked the questions in the exercise, she found out that the metal strip represented the burden she was experiencing in relation to her daughter. Her daughter was old enough now to handle her own problems, but the mother had held onto the habit of being responsible for her daughter's decisions and actions. What a relief when she separated out the love for her daughter and placed it in her heart, and buried the rest.

Another mother experienced the guilt she held onto concerning her children, only it was a hard ball in her stomach. For her it was also a relief to let it go.

A businessman experienced his fear of proceeding on a certain project as a thorn in his side. The thorn, on closer examination, indicated a fear of expressing his ideas to one person in his department. After releasing the thorn, communication proceeded, and the project moved ahead.

Other images have ranged from chains around the neck to a prickly feeling all over the skin. As with every exercise, some people will experience intense feelings, while others will visualize the whole thing, and others still will be partially thinking, musing and allowing thoughts about a situation to float to the surface of their mind. Trust your own experience.

## The Medium is Not the Message

Here again, we find examples of the images or feelings or sensations triggering an internal knowing. It is important to recognize that the images and impressions are not Intuition; they just bring the intuitive knowing to the conscious mind. Most of us need such a trigger, at least in the beginning. Some of us do not, or need them less, as our relationship with our Intuition improves.

* * * * *

### DAILY EXERCISES:

For the first three days, repeat the above exercise using different types of fears and anxieties. For instance:

**DAY ONE:** Explore a fear about the future.

**DAY TWO:** Explore a fear that concerns someone you love.

**DAY THREE:** Explore a fear that you had in the past, and do not necessarily still have.

**DAY FOUR to DAY SEVEN:** Try something new each day, something you have been reluctant or uncomfortable about trying before, such as learning a new skill, trying a type of food you have not eaten before, travelling a new route to work, or to the store, or to wherever you may be going today. Let yourself try something new. Even if you never do the thing again, or never eat the food again, you have broken a Fear Barrier about something. This will make it easier to recognize a fear – and release it – the next time.

\* \* \* \* \*

We all have likes and dislikes, but we also have things we don't try because we don't think we'll like them, or don't think we'll be able to do them well. These are little fears that can undermine our self-trust and confidence. By disciplining ourselves to break through some of these little fears, it becomes easier to understand and put into perspective our bigger fears.

## Fear vs. Danger

The final reminder about fear is to remember that "the only thing to fear is fear itself." Fear is a natural part of being human, but it can paralyze us if we give it too much of our power. If we can keep it in perspective we will recognize the difference between fear and danger.

Danger is something that is an immediate experience. It has to do with the present. We may notice a leak in the gas pipe and recognize it as dangerous, or we may be driving in a snow storm and recognize that we need to be careful. These are really dangers that need to be noticed and appreciated for what they are.

Fear usually revolves around a future we cannot know, based on a past that has already happened. When there is nothing you can do about a situation right now, fear is useless and a waste of energy. You can recognize danger and take precautions, but fear merely drains and paralyzes you.

## Intuition Directs

Intuition remains neutral in these experiences. Using Intuition, then, is a part of recognizing danger. The part of your mind that directs your attention to the frayed electrical wire, or to the memory of an iron left on, is part of your Intuition. But if you are always afraid that you left something on, when your history indicates that you have not, it is simply a case of your fearful mindset undermining you, draining your energy.

Have you ever been in an emergency situation and just automatically acted? Later on you may have reacted emotionally and got the shakes, as you thought about what **could** have happened. But in the moment you responded instinctively, without thinking. After the emergency is over, your mind has a chance to bring up all its fears and anxieties. But the real situation has passed.

Fears that we experience **before** doing something can be seen in the same way. Since an emergency isn't really in the offing, we have plenty of time to let our fears subdue our instincts.

These are the kinds of situations in which listening to your Intuition can keep you on track, and help you deal with the fears for what they are: nothing substantial, just fear.

# CHAPTER
# 5

## -WEEK FOUR-
## Trusting Your Intuition, Part II
## Understanding Desire

*Once upon a crossroad a poor Poet met a rich*
*Stupid, and they conversed. And all that they said*
*revealed their discontent.*

*Then the Angel of the Road passed by, and he*
*laid his hand upon the shoulders of the two men.*
*And behold, a miracle: the two men had now*
*exchanged their possessions.*

*And they parted. But strange to relate, the*
*Poet looked and found naught in his hand but dry*
*moving sand; and the Stupid closed his eyes and*
*felt naught but a cloud moving in his heart.*
*— Kahlil Gibran*

## Strengthen What is Weak

Last week and this week are real workouts. After loos-
ening up the first couple of weeks, we are now into deep
training. In other words, we are getting at the root of why

59

Intuition does not seem to work for most people who have not trained their Intuitive Muscle.

Dealing with our fears and our desires and looking at how they interfere with Intuition is similar to exercising the weakest part of our body. It hurts sometimes, and there is a strong tendency to avoid it, because it is weak.

It is no fun to admit that we are not perfect. When part of us is quite strong, why develop what is weak? When we find the courage to strengthen what is weak, even our strong parts function better, because they are supported by the whole of us, rather than doing the job by themselves. It is the same with Intuition. When the Intuitive Muscle is strengthened, our whole decision-making process is strengthened.

Our desires are as strong as our fears, and they both weaken our ability to listen and trust our Intuition.

## Goals vs. Desires

Not all desire interferes with Intuition. Wanting something to happen can influence where we direct our energies. It thus encourages the things we want to happen. An inspiration or idea can become a type of desire that directs us toward achieving a goal. These types of desire are beneficial because they motivate us to go beyond our normal limits.

However, there is a type of desire that can short-circuit us. Sometimes our desire interferes with our normal functioning, or focuses on something that we have no control over attaining. This type of desire clouds our ability to deal with the present. For example, we can desire to have the perfect body; but this desire makes it difficult to accept who we are, if our bones happen to be bigger than our image of perfect, or if we put off doing something that is important to us until our body is perfect.

Examples of this are: "I will look for that new job when I'm looking good," or "When I get the recognition I deserve, I will be ready to commit to a relationship." That kind of desire undermines our confidence and self-esteem. It is a way of short-circuiting ourselves into not doing what is important to us. This kind of desire is just a cover-up for a fear of success.

## Desire Can Cloud Your Thinking

When we become too attached to seeing only what we think is good for us, or what we want to see, we stop thinking clearly and stop using our own common sense.

For myself, my own desire to have the "perfect birth" for my first child clouded my ability to listen to my Intuition. I had a vision of a breech birth a few days before delivery, but since I didn't want that to happen, I dismissed it and did not prepare for it. I knew that the "perfect" birth was a normal, vaginal delivery, and I did not want anything else.

Guess what? My first child was breech. It was one of those times when I knew it, but did not listen because of my desire for what I considered perfection.

Even now, after years of teaching Intuition, when I go to the grocery store and just want to go home, I do not listen to my Intuition. When some item catches my eye, I should just pick it up, because if I do not, when I get home I invariably find that indeed we needed that item, even though it was not on the shopping list. I should know better, and when I do not listen, it reinforces how right Intuition is, and how desires often interfere.

## Desire as a Distortion of Inspiration

The type of desire that ends up interfering with our Intuition is the one that usually comes from a true inspiration, but then gets identified with a specific set of circumstances, which causes us to lose track of the original inspiration.

Let's look again at the example of my first child's birth. The original inspiration was to have a healthy child. I defined "having a healthy child" as a natural birth with no complications.

My specific definition made me unwilling to listen to my Intuition, which also had the original inspiration and indicated steps to take to insure it. The original inspiration usually implies that we, as individuals, need to grow and change in order to fulfill its promise. This is part of the natural creative process.

## Growth and Inspiration

If we knew how to do something already, there would be no challenge in it, and it would not be creative. When we get an idea, and when it becomes something we want to accomplish, it always requires us to change, to learn something fresh, to do something in a new way. Most of us have probably had the feeling that "if I had known what was going to be involved, I never would have done it." Whether we jump or walk carefully into a new situation, it always has surprises and turns for us. That is how it should be, because that is how we grow and change.

A student of mine wanted a committed relationship. He defined that as a partnership with a person with specific attributes. His definition of who it should be kept him from recognizing someone who did come into his life, someone who could care deeply for him and vice versa. He was too busy judging that person's superficial qualities to notice how he was feeling about her. His original inspiration was inviting him to explore his feelings, and to try to trust his feelings. Instead of changing, he limited the original inspiration to a set of mentally defined qualities he was looking for.

Since it is our wanting something that interferes with Intuition, the main exercise for this week is about what it feels like to let go of what we think we want. We also explore what it feels like to really get what we want and to rediscover the original inspiration behind it.

* * * * *

## MAIN EXERCISE:
## UNDERSTANDING DESIRE

For this exercise, think about something that you want. Since the purpose of this exercise is to help you understand your desire and how it interferes with listening to your Intuition, pick something that you really want, something that you know you desire. You will need about 20 quiet minutes for this exercise.

*Make yourself comfortable. Close your eyes and take a few deep breaths. Breathe deeply, letting go of all distractions and thoughts. Practice letting your whole body breathe. Imagine yourself as a balloon. Every time you inhale, the balloon which is your body expands, bringing vital, sparkling, energizing air into you. Every time you*

63

HARMON

exhale, the balloon which is your body deflates, letting go
of tensions, distractions, and thoughts.

 

*Now, go into the environment where you met your
Intuition. Take a few moments to get yourself there.
Notice your surroundings. Is there anything you would
like to change? Is there anything new here? Take a few
moments to make yourself comfortable.*

*Invite in your Intuition. Say "Hello," and ask if there is
anything Intuition would like to communicate to you right
now.*

*Present your Intuition with your desire, the thing or
event you really want in your life. Let Intuition create an
image that represents what you desire. Perhaps your
Intuition is holding this image, or perhaps your Intuition
becomes the symbol itself, or perhaps the symbol becomes
something in the environment. Whatever it is represented
by is not as important as having it represented by something – even a vague smoky or cloudy substance.*

*Ask your Intuition and yourself the following ques-
tions. Remember to let the answers come as feelings,
words, images, thoughts, or however they are communicated to you. And if you do not get an answer to one question, do not dwell on it. Just go on to the next one.*

*If this event or thing did not happen or appear in your
life, how would you feel? How would that affect what you
are doing now in your life?*

*How does wanting this interfere with your present life?
Are there any other feelings associated with this desire?
Is there a fear that this desire is covering up?
What happens when you do not get what you want?
What do you enjoy about not getting what you want?
Is there a deeper longing that this desire represents to*

*you? In other words, what do you really want? What was the original inspiration?*

*What would have to change if you got what you wanted? Spend a few moments really pretending that you got what you wanted. Let it sink in. Spend some time imagining the different circumstances in your life right now, and how it would really change if you got what you wanted. How does it feel? Are you happy? Are there any new problems to deal with?*

*Take as much time as you need to ponder these questions, and let your Intuition help you find the answers.*

*Perhaps you are having difficulty experiencing how it would feel to get what you want, or in letting go of what you want. If so, take the symbol and put it inside of you. What would it feel like to really have it? Let yourself fully experience what it feels like.*

*Now take it out and let it go. See what it feels like to really let it go.*

*What do you now know about your desire?*

*Thank your Intuition and let your Intuition leave this environment for now. Take a few deep breaths, and prepare yourself for leaving. Bring yourself back into the room you are sitting in and open your eyes. Record your experience in your journal.*

* * * * *

## Examples

For the person discussed earlier, the man who wanted a "committed relationship," this exercise helped him understand that for him, keeping open emotionally, and staying tuned to what he was feeling was more important than comparing everyone he met to a list of qualities. Staying in touch with his feelings was not going to be as easy as keeping the list in mind, but it would bring him closer to his goal.

Another student wanted freedom. She defined freedom as having enough money to do whatever she wanted. So she was constantly figuring out ways to make more money, but she never had enough, and always felt trapped by her circumstances.

She understood, after the above exercise, that the freedom she wanted had to do with feeling free right now, free to do the things in her life that would nurture her, even if she had to keep on working for money in the meantime. It made her very uncomfortable to think about really giving herself inner freedom. She recognized that it wouldn't happen overnight, but now she can hear more clearly what her Intuition is saying, even if she decides to do something differently. She is making the choice. She is no longer a victim of her circumstances.

In choosing a situation to use in this exercise, one student used her desire to lose weight. She experienced the desire as a sticky, elastic, stretchy substance that was dark brown, and it stuck to both of her hands.

Her Intuition told her just to get rid of it. But she did not know how. I interpreted it as follows: she needed to get rid of the whole desire to lose weight. That desire was a real nuisance. She was not sure about this: letting go of desire can be a very difficult thing, especially when our self-image is involved. It is hard to let go of things that are tied up with what we think we want to be or to look like.

* * * * *

## DAILY EXERCISES:

**DAY ONE to DAY THREE:** Review the main exercise, and try it with different wants and desires.

**DAY FOUR to DAY FIVE:** Remember a time in your life when you *did* get what you wanted. Write down the story that goes with it. Were you satisfied? Was your deeper longing also fulfilled? How did you have to change during the process? What did you learn from that experience? And how can that experience help you understand your present desires?

One way that we can tell the difference between an inspiration and a desire is to look at what we accomplish in our lives, and what we leave undone. We all have many ideas that occur to us as potential possibilities. Some of these we are motivated to take action on and complete. In other cases, we retain the idea, but the event never happens. The things we actually accomplish are inspirations which have motivated us. Other ideas just pass through. They occur to us once, and then we think no more about them.

Some ideas nag us and are recurring, but we do not take action on them. We want them, but never do anything to truly make them happen. These are the desires that we want to examine more closely. They can drain our energy and distract us from other, more fulfilling activities.

This exercise is designed to help you look a little more closely at what ideas and inspirations have motivated you, and which ones have turned into draining desires.

**DAY SIX to DAY SEVEN:** Make a list of all the things you want. Write down next to each item how getting it would change your life, both in the things that would be added and the things that would have to be released. Reflect on how willing you are to change that much!

* * * * *

## Courage

By now you may be feeling exhausted. This phase of the Intuition workout corresponds to the phase in a physical workout where you have pushed yourself beyond your perceived limits. You now realize how out-of-shape you are and consider giving up. Your thoughts may run something like: "I can't do this." "I'm in terrible shape." "I've got so far to go; what is the point?"

Now is not the time to give up, although it does take courage to face your fears and your desires. An Intuition workout is not as fun at this point, but with courage and perseverance you will gain confidence.

Remember that courage is the ability to go on and take action even when you feel afraid or unsure. Acknowledge to yourself what hard work this is, how unpleasant it can be, and keep going. You can do it!

# 6

# -WEEK FIVE-
## Building Confidence

*William Durant would proceed on a course of action guided solely, as far as I could tell, by some intuitive flash of brilliance. He never felt obligated to make an engineering hunt for the facts.*
*—Alfred P. Sloan, former chairman of General Motors*

Whew! Getting through those last two chapters can be a bit rough on your sense of self. Now that you have got a few of the cobwebs out of your system, you can go back to some of the Intuition exercises you tried before and find out how strong your Intuitive Muscle has become.

## Developing Your Style

By now you may be starting to sense your personal style. Perhaps your Intuition communicates to you in a particular way or with a special feeling, or perhaps a similar sensation comes over you whenever you flex your

Intuitive Muscle. Once your personal method emerges, you can build your confidence by observing and perfecting it.

This chapter is about defining your personal style, expanding it and trusting it. Once you begin to realize that the way you make decisions is a little or a lot different from anyone else, you are 75% through your training. When you try to make decisions like someone else, no matter how successful they may be, it is not your way. You can learn from someone, and incorporate what is successful for them into your style, but just to imitate someone is the kiss of death for your Intuition.

Intuition is always individual. Aspects may be similar to those of someone else, but the nature of Intuition is an inner experience, a sense of self that emerges outward into our personal life. So, the more you understand who you are – how you are different from others, and how you are the same – the more connected you will be to your Intuition.

## Self-confidence Supports Intuition

What builds confidence in Intuition is a strong sense of your uniqueness. Someone who is not sure of themselves will be more likely to doubt their Intuition, or only follow it half-heartedly. Someone with self-confidence will follow their Intuition with a sense of sureness. The main exercise of this chapter is designed to acquaint you with yourself and your Intuition. The daily exercises expand that feeling and apply it to the situations in your life.

For this exercise sit down and make yourself comfortable. You will need about 10 minutes of uninterrupted time.

* * * * *

## MAIN EXERCISE:
## THE BUBBLE

*Close your eyes and take a few deep breaths. Let each breath bring in sparkling, luminous energy. Let each exhalation release the tensions of the day, the thoughts, the distractions. Keep breathing deeply, letting energy in and tension out.*

*Begin to imagine that you are completely surrounded by a bubble. Make sure that this bubble does not cramp you, but is perfectly comfortable. It is just the right size for*

73

you. It's not too big, and not too small, with plenty of room for you to breathe. Make sure that the bubble goes under your feet and over your head.

This bubble is made of a substance so strong that no outside energies can enter in. Make sure it is thick enough to guarantee this. It can still be clear, but it is strong and thick.

Inside the bubble there is only your energy. It emanates out from you and bounces against the inside of the bubble. Then it comes back to you. Being in the bubble magnifies what it feels like to be you. All you have to do is relax and breathe, and feel the bubble around you.

Your energy keeps bouncing back to you and keeps getting stronger. You may even begin to sense a rhythm to your energy, or perhaps some colors that are associated with it. You may hear a sound or sounds that correspond to your energy. Your energy may have a texture, or thickness to it. Whatever it is, sense it and absorb it, and let yourself become comfortable with it.

Spend as much time as your would like to here in your bubble. When you are ready to leave, let the image of the bubble fade away, but retain the feeling of your energy. Keep it with you all day. If you forget about it, remember the bubble, and the feeling will come right back. When you are ready, you can open your eyes. Record your experiences in your journal.

* * * * *

This exercise is usually quite refreshing. It provides a time and a way to relax into yourself and get to know who you are. Some people are surprised by what they experience. They might have thought that they were a calm, easy-going person, but discover in the bubble how much energy and drive they really have.

Others are surprised at how much of who they thought they were is based on what other people expected from them. When they finally get access to their own personal energy, they find that places where there was tension are now relaxed; where there was worry, there is now joy.

I remember one student who first experienced her energy as sticky. After a few moments in the bubble, the stickiness disappeared. When she thought about it, she realized that she "sticks" to people in order to feel more secure. Once she let herself be herself, the stickiness was gone.

This insight did not transform her life overnight. But by realizing that she defined herself by what others thought of her, and by developing a sense of *self* – awareness of which increased through this exercise – she was able to become comfortable with her own presence.

## Getting From Insight to Change

The moment of insight can be wonderful. At that point we get a glimpse of what has been and what could be, all at the same time. After the insight we may expect the change to happen spontaneously and sometimes it does. It is more common, however, that change happens over a period of time. During this time we may experience turmoil. While our minds may be able to change instantly, our habits and the world around us usually move at a slower pace and it takes a little time and practice to catch up. So, do not be hard on yourself if things don't change immediately. Be understanding and persistent with your-self, your habits, and the people around you.

* * * * *

## DAILY EXERCISES:

**DAY TWO:** *Sit down and make yourself comfortable. Close your eyes and breathe deeply for a few moments. Let yourself breathe in vitality, and exhale tension. Remember your bubble. Let it surround you.*

*Notice if it has changed at all since the last time you did this exercise. Breathe deeply while you are in the bubble. Remember that the bubble is strong and thick enough to keep all energies except your own out of the bubble. As you breathe, feel yourself breathing your own energy in and out. Become comfortable with your energy, with what it feels like to be you.*

*Now, think of someone you know. Someone you feel comfortable with in your life. Someone you like. Imagine them in their own bubble, and let them float towards you. What kind of bubble do they have? What kind of energy is in it? Take a few moments to observe them in their bubble and reflect on how different or similar your energies are.*

*Now let your bubbles merge. Let your energies blend with each other. Notice how you respond. How does your energy change? How does the other person's energy change? Are you still comfortable? Are you uncomfortable? Have you lost a sense of your self? Has the other person lost their sense of self?*

*Let the two bubbles become separate again. Thank your friend for doing this with you and let their bubble float away.*

*Remain in your bubble for a few moments, feeling what it feels like to be just you again.*

*When you are ready, you can let the image of the bubble disappear, and open your eyes. Record your experience in your journal.*

\* \* \* \* \*

This exercise can be very informative. I remember one student who, when she did this exercise, felt her bubble wrapping around the other person. She felt how she loses her sense of self, especially around a man she is romantically interested in. She had known this before, but this exercise let her see it, and to feel how tiring it was for her. After this, she began to take steps to feel more consistently herself, even with someone she was involved with.

Another student experienced how powerful her energy was. She had been told by other people how strong she was, but she never believed it. This exercise made clear to her what she puts out in the world. It encouraged her not to be afraid of it, but to use it wisely.

Someone else felt very uncomfortable in her bubble. At first she did not think she could get enough air in her bubble. She said of herself: "I know my energy is strong and bright and the thought of confining it was a little uncomfortable at first. I then realized I could be in a brilliant bubble of confined space but my energy could extend outside of the bubble like a multitude of sun rays. I was then quite happy inside. I felt I had excess energy." She then went on to do all the bubble exercises and found them very revealing of some of her relationship patterns.

\* \* \* \* \*

**DAY THREE:** Repeat the above exercise with

someone you do not feel so comfortable around: someone who bothers you, or gets on your nerves, or someone you are temporarily angry with.

**DAY FOUR:** Repeat the above exercise with someone else, either someone you are comfortable or uncomfortable with.

**DAY FIVE:** Today, think of a situation you are in, one in which you would like some guidance from your Intuition. Then do the following exercise.

### BUBBLE, WITH A SPECIFIC SITUATION:

*Make yourself comfortable, close your eyes and breathe.*

*Remember your bubble, and let it surround you. By now this is getting easy. Remember the feeling in your bubble. Has it changed? Has your level of comfort with it changed?*

*Take a few moments to let yourself breathe in your energy, without interference. Let go to it.*

*Now, think of a particular situation in your life that you would like some guidance on. Let the situation float towards you in its own bubble. What does it look like in there? How does it feel? What colors, textures, smells, shapes seem to be associated with it?*

*Just by looking at this situation, you may get an impression that will help you understand and approach it. You can now let your two bubbles merge. How does that feel? What does it tell you about this situation, and your involvement with it?*

*When you are ready, you can let the bubbles separate. Let the bubble with the situation in it float away.*

*Take a few more deep breaths and let your bubble fade away.*

*Open your eyes and write down your experience in your journal.*

**\* \* \* \* \***

A situation on which I tried this exercise was the writing of this book. When I saw the book in its bubble, it fell out and dropped down. This gave me the feeling that the book was too heavy. However hard I tried lifting the book up in order to put it back in its bubble, it would not stay. It kept dropping down.

I began to think about ways in which I could lighten up the book – make it more fun and not so heavy. As I did this, the book lightened up and stayed in its bubble. I knew, then, what I had to do to improve the book, and, of course, I did it!

When I blended the book's bubble and my own, an explosion took place. I felt the excitement and the energy. I knew then this book would be successful. Wishful thinking? Maybe, so I did the desire exercise, and let the success go. I can let it go: certainly I want the book to be successful, but that is not what I am writing it for. If it gives people a way to increase their understanding of the value of their Intuition, I'll be happy.

**DAY SIX:** Repeat the above exercise with another situation or decision.

**DAY SEVEN:** Try staying in your bubble all day. That does not mean that you have to keep your eyes closed all day. Just keep the feeling of the bubble around you as much as you can. Keep remembering that it is there. Notice how you feel, how people react to you, if your sense of self changes, or if you behavior changes. Be sure to write your results in your journal.

* * * * *

## Back to Intuition

You may be asking yourself right now, "What do bubbles, personal energy, and how I feel about others have to do with Intuition?" That is a good question, and there is a good answer to go with it. At the beginning of the chapter I spoke about confidence, and how confidence in oneself makes listening to one's Intuition easier. Let's go back to that concept for a few moments.

Confidence is the ability to be comfortable with yourself, whether you are right or wrong, whether you need to go ahead with something or let it go. Whatever has to be done or understood can be done with assurance and without self-judgment.

## Judgment Undermines Confidence

Once we begin to judge ourselves as being successes or failures when circumstances and situations around us succeed or fail, we lose confidence. We then have to shield ourselves from what we would consider failures, or mistakes. We have to bolster up our successes. We have then stopped seeing ourselves as whole, and we have blocked off our ability to listen to our Intuition when it says something we find it difficult to accept.

Becoming comfortable with ourselves means becoming comfortable with *all* of ourselves, warts and all: mistakes and successes, challenges and defeats. This chapter is designed to increase your confidence in you – whoever or whatever that is. Your Intuition, making no judgments, remaining neutral, can then freely communicate to you.

Take the above example of myself, writing this book. If I had been extremely attached to what I had already written, and felt that too much revision would mean I was a failure, I would have disregarded my Intuition. I would have blocked it off, and not seen what it was communicating to me.

We all need to take stock of ourselves from time to time. With a truthful, neutral attitude toward ourselves, we can focus on how we can change to improve ourselves. As Pat Rodegast says in Emmanual's Book, "We are perfectly imperfect."

To me this means that we are perfect at all times, with room to grow and change and develop at the same time. We do not expect a first grader to understand calculus. In the same way we ought to accept ourselves in our unfinished state.

Have fun!

# 7

## -WEEK SIX-
## Our Expert Mind

*Five major steel companies advised me to use harder materials for the containers, dies, tooling, and so forth. Instead, I decided that softer tooling was the better answer. Our president directed me to abide by the decision of the major steel mills. Nevertheless, I followed my own Intuition and spent two-and-a-half times more money for the softer material. The result was an outstanding success with the softer tooling. It lasts six times as long as harder steels. The entire industry has now followed this procedure.*

—Richard Haupt
(While executive vice-president of Electric Hydracon Co.)

* * *

*Don't worry about your difficulties in mathematics, I can assure you that mine are still greater.*
—Albert Einstein

There is one last major obstacle that keeps you from listening to your Intuition. I know that you have it, because everyone does. It is the part of our mind that knows it all – the part that has decided what is going to happen, when it is going to happen and what the outcome will be. It is called the Expert Mind.

If you have driven the same way to work every day for 15 years, you know the way, right? You know what is going to happen, right? You don't even have to pay attention anymore. Your body knows the way, right? Right – and wrong! What happened today when you drove to work? Are you aware of that time? Did you make good use of it, or was it lost time?

Now think back to the first time you drove to that location. I bet you paid close attention to every detail! You can probably remember that day because it is so etched in your mind.

Think about the first time you drove a car. You probably do not remember every time you have driven a car, but you remember something about the first time. That is because the first time you were *present* in everything that went on. You watched and noticed everything. You were in the state opposite to the Expert Mind. You were in Beginners Mind.

## Expert Minds Know Everything

We have all had experiences with the Expert Minds of others. Remember the college professor who would not listen to your great idea because it was...impossible! out of the question! He or she already knew it all. After all, they had studied for years. They had earned a Ph.D. They were expert in their field. *But as soon as someone assumes they know it all, they have stopped learning*. The door that allows more information in, perhaps even a change of mind, closes. Learning stops. There is no room for more information that might conflict with what is already known.

Whenever a new theory explains phenomena in terms different from those currently accepted, it takes years and years of frustration and even persecution to win a hearing – remember Galileo and Columbus? Expert minds slow the process of evolution, because they are resistant to anything new. Part of all our minds is Expert Mind.

## Zen and the Art of Beginners Mind

This whole concept of Expert Mind/Beginners Mind is a Zen approach to living which can be applied quite easily to the study of Intuition. A story that illustrates this concerns a scholarly man who wanted to study with a Zen monk.

This man went to the monk and told of his desire to learn about and study Zen. The monk asked the man to sit down for tea. The man continued to talk about what he knew, thinking he needed to impress the monk with his knowledge before the monk would accept him as a student. As the man was repeating how important it was for him to learn Zen, and how much he already knew about other religions, the monk poured the man some tea.

But the monk did not stop pouring tea. The man's cup started overflowing. The tea ran over the cup and onto the floor. The man stopped talking and asked the monk what he was doing. The monk replied that the cup was like the man's mind. It was overflowing with knowledge. How

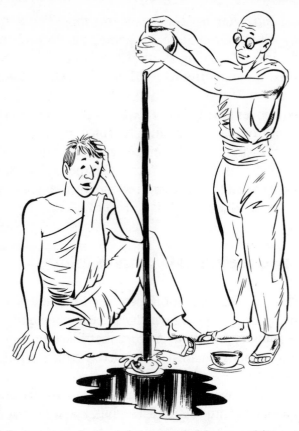

could he expect the monk to teach him anything, when there was no room for any more knowledge? "Before we can learn anything," said the monk, "we have to have an empty mind."

The Beginners Mind is the empty mind. It means that we do everything we do as if it were the first time we were doing it. We bring to it the freshness and alertness of the first time, because truly we are doing it for the first time. It is the first time on this particular day, when we are a particular age, both of which will never occur again.

With Beginners Mind, we can appreciate the beauty of

each moment, and be alert to what is happening this particular time, even with something we have done a million times before. How can actors and singers do a Broadway show thousands of times, eight or ten shows a week, and be fresh and new each time? They have to remember that it is the first and probably only time this particular audience is here, and make it their first time too.

## Applying Beginners Mind to our Lives

Only a Beginners Mind can be successful at that kind of routine. How can those of us who go to the same job, at the same desk or station every day, make it new each time? Isn't that asking an awful lot of us? Perhaps it is asking a lot, because it is asking us to live our lives fully, to make every moment count and to be present in what is happening right now.

It is also asking us to be responsible for making our life interesting. Rather than waiting to be entertained by life, it is up to us to open our minds to the newness and excitement that is there, every day, no matter how many times we have done the same thing in the same place.

The magic of Beginners Mind is that anyone can do it! It does not take years of education, but years of education do not hinder us. A simple act of opening our minds to the present moment does it every time. Instead of assuming that this Monday is going to be like every other Monday, focus on the date. It is the only Monday, February 23, 1990 that will ever be. So be open to what the day will bring, and what *you* can bring to the day.

## Beginners Mind and the Present Moment

In order to be in Beginner's Mind we have to be in the present moment. If we are too concerned with the past, assuming that the past is going to repeat itself over and over again, it will! And we will be bored. Being concerned about the future is the same thing as preoccupation with the past. The future is either our hope or fear that the past will repeat itself.

This doesn't mean we don't have goals or direction in life. We can have direction and still live in the present moment. The state I'm talking about is when the present is consumed by the past and the future. This is the case when what we are doing right now is overwhelmed by our thoughts about the past and/or future.

For example, I knew someone who worked in a job she could not stand. It really was causing her to be sick, tired, bored and frustrated. The job was not suited to her, nor was it challenging. She was not even doing the job effectively. But my friend kept talking about what was going to happen someday. This job was going to lead her into the position she really wanted.

Guess what happened? She finally got the job she wanted. It was not what she expected! It, too, was not the right job for her – what a waste of the present, for a future as yet undetermined.

## Opportunities for Beginners Mind

Now we all have to do things that aren't our favorite things to do in order to accomplish our goals. We make decisions and judgments based on what is important to us.

Washing the dishes is not one of my favorite chores in life, but I do do it. Sometimes I really do not want to take the dog for a walk, but it needs to be done. These are opportunities for me to practice Beginner's Mind.

Beginners mind brings us back to the present moment and can be useful anytime. Beginners Mind does not mean that we forget the past, but that our focus is on the present and we can draw upon the past and future when necessary. Beginners Mind means that we are not overpowered by the past and future.

The story about my friend is about living for the future. In this state we are waiting for the Big Something to happen, and we put the rest of our lives on hold until it does. If my friend had practiced Beginners Mind during this time in his life, at least two possibilities could have emerged. He could have begun to enjoy his present job, making the most of what challenges were there, or he might have realized that he was wasting his time there and looked for a more fulfilling job or career. Of course, something else altogether might have happened. With Beginners Mind you never know!

Living in the present is recognizing that the dishes need to be done, or the dog needs a walk, and doing it, finding something to enjoy about it, and being present to what needs to be done.

## Intuition and the Present Moment

In order to listen to our Intuition, we need to recognize Beginners Mind and Expert Mind. When we are so sure about what is going to happen, or what needs to happen, that we squeeze out the present moment, it is difficult to allow other possibilities to occur.

Richard Haupt, who was quoted at the beginning of this chapter, had to release his Expert Mind, and the expert minds around him, in order to try something new. That something new cost a lot of money and required an incredible amount of risk and guts. The Expert Mind in all of us cannot allow the new, creative idea to emerge. If it does not fit in with what has been done over and over again, it says, "Forget it. It will never work."

Intuition is *always* in the present moment, and will always give us a fresh approach to an old situation. We need to discipline our Expert Mind in order to appreciate what our Intuition is telling us.

## Beginners Mind Keeps Us Present

To summarize, we all have an Expert Mind and a Beginners Mind. It is a matter of where we put our attention that switches us from one to the other. The Expert Mind is concerned with the past and the future. It focuses on what has been done before, and what will probably happen based on past experience.

The Beginners Mind stays in the present. It is involved with what is happening as if it were the first time. The Beginners Mind then allows new approaches and insights to occur. Creativity and innovation are spontaneous with the Beginners Mind. Our Intuition is associated with the Beginners Mind, because in order to listen to Intuition we have to be open to whatever is appropriate, not relying on what has been done a million times before and is "always" the right way to proceed.

Our Expert Mind hinders and restricts our Intuition. Our Beginners Mind stays open to what our Intuition would like to communicate.

There are three main exercises for this week. The first one has to do with encouraging our Beginners Mind, finding the switch in our mind that turns off the Expert and turns on the Beginner. The second main exercise has to do with releasing ourselves from the past and the future, so we can concentrate on remaining in the present moment. The final one gives us practice in remaining neutral in difficult situations or with difficult people.

With all of these exercises, our awareness is the key factor. When we catch ourselves being bored, it is easy to turn it around and start looking for what could be interesting. If we do not catch ourselves, we can get dragged down into feeling victimized by our circumstances, and trapped in a situation.

Our body is always present. Our mind can travel anywhere. It can go back to the past just by remembering something and into the future by wondering what is going to happen. Our mind can be right here or 10 blocks away, visiting someone we know by thinking about them.

Our body is always present. It is our body that cannot leave now to go somewhere else. If your involvement with the past and the future is keeping you from being present to the moment, try thinking about your toes, or arms, or any part of your body, or center your awareness in your breath. That will bring you back to the present.

* * * * *

**CORE EXERCISES:**

**DAY ONE:** Take a few moments to reflect on your Expert Mind and your Beginners Mind. Feel the difference. Think of a particular situation in your life right now.

How does your Expert Mind approach it? How does your
Beginners Mind approach it? Create a switch in your mind
that turns on the Beginners Mind and turns off the Expert
Mind. Play with that switch and become aware of what
changes in you. Use your Beginners Mind on some task
that you do every day. Write your thoughts and experiences in your journal.

**DAY TWO to DAY FIVE:** Write down several
areas in your life in which you feel quite competent. Write
down what you know about them, and how you deal with
situations that apply what you know. You can summarize
and just write the major points. Pick one of these areas that
has a present application in your life. Perhaps there is a situation at work or home which requires your expertise.

This week, I want you to talk to someone you do not
consider an expert on this subject. Tell them the situation,
and ask for their opinion and their advice. It is important
that you keep your Beginners Mind tuned in to what they
tell you. Listen with as open a mind as you can muster.
Incorporate their ideas into your expertise. See if you can
learn something new about something you know a lot
about this week.

### DAY THREE & FOUR:
### RELEASING PAST & FUTURE

*Sit down and make yourself comfortable. You will
need about 15 minutes of uninterrupted time to complete
this exercise. Take a few moments to breathe deeply. As
you inhale, breathe in sparkling, luminous energy which
brings in vitality. Exhale, releasing the thoughts of the
day, the tensions, the distractions.*

*Go to the environment where you first met your*

*Intuition. Take a few moments to feel yourself there. Has
anything changed? Is there anything you would like to
change?*

*Find a place to sit down and relax. Make yourself com-
fortable here. Enjoy the peaceful serenity of this place.*

*Continue breathing deeply, and as you do, imagine that
the part of you that is involved with the past begins to
drain out of you. Feel it being released, and as it is
released, let it gather on one side of you. As it is released
from you, let it gather and become formed into some substance. It may be quite vague and smoky; that is just fine.
It may be quite solid and distinct; that is OK too. Focus on
letting all of your involvement with the past drain out of
you.*

*How does it feel to be rid of the past, for just these few
moments?*

*Now, let all of your involvement with the future drain
out of you. Feel it draining and forming on the other side
of you. Sense the form that the future takes as it drains out
of you.*

*How does it feel to be rid of the future for just these
few moments?*

*Take a few moments to focus on the past and future, as
they remain outside of you. How do they feel? Is one
stronger than the other? Is one more formed than the other?
Does one feel heavier than the other? Let your hands reach
out and push against the past and the future. Make sure
that they are out there and not in you.*

*Now, focus on the present moment, on what is left in
you. How does it feel to be present?*

*Think of some situation in your life that is troubling
you. Bring that situation into your mind right now. How*

*would you approach the situation from the perspective of the present moment? How much of your situation is based in the past or future? Let yourself gain the perspective of the present moment .*

*What can you learn about this situation, and what new approaches are available to you from this perspective?*

*Take as much time as you need to reflect on what you have learned.*

*When you are ready, bring as much as you want of the past and future back into you. Leave the rest outside of you.*

*Prepare to leave this place. When you are ready, take a few deep breaths and open your eyes. Record your experiences in your journal.*

\* \* \* \* \*

## Experiences

This exercise has produced some interesting results. One student experienced the past as a dark cloud that kept pulling him back. The future was a bright cloud, also pulling, but forward. The troubling situation he considered was clouded over by the past. The present moment provided a solution that was not based on the fear that the past would repeat itself.

Another student was dominated by the future. Her future was always brighter than the present. Nothing could compete with the wonderful future, and most situations in the present were disappointing. When she released herself from the future for a few moments, the present became filled with opportunities to enjoy, without waiting for the future.

**DAY FOUR & DAY FIVE:** Practice being present, and exercising your Beginners Mind.

## Practicing Neutrality

**DAY SIX:** Beginners Mind can also be a Neutral Mind. When our emotional and intellectual responses lock us into certain behavior patterns, the following two exercises can be helpful. Practicing neutrality is also important when our emotional and intellectual attachments to a particular outcome cloud our ability to sense what our Intuition is communicating to us.

This exercise is designed to be done with someone in mind who gets on your nerves. These are the most difficult people for us to be neutral with, so we use them for this exercise.

I suggest that you try the following exercise first with someone who is not central in your life right now, but someone who gets on your nerves. We have all had the experience of being bothered by someone, without really knowing why. For some reason, the way they walk, dress, talk, or relate gets on our nerves and we can't seem to communicate clearly with them. Our feelings keep getting in the way.

Take a few moments to think of whom you want to use, then sit down and get comfortable.

* * * * *

PRACTICING NEUTRALITY

*Close your eyes, relax thoroughly, and take a few deep breaths.*

*Begin to imagine that this person is sitting in front of*

*you. Remember as many details about them as possible. Their eyes, their hair, their clothes, how they hold their body. Think of as many little features of them as you can.*

*Really* **feel** *them in front of you. Imagine their image in front of you. If you do not visualize very well, that is all right. Sense their presence in front of you. How does it feel to be in their presence?*

*Now, imagine that there is a large piece of glass between the two of you. This glass must be thick enough to keep you from responding to this person the way you normally do. You can still see each other through the glass, but do not respond to each other in your usual way. You can observe this person through the glass, and you can observe your reactions to this person.*

*Take a few moments to get this picture firmly in your mind. The person you have chosen is on the opposite side of a thick pane of glass.*

*Once the glass is in place, put a thermometer on the glass to one side of the person. Make sure that you can still see the person clearly, and the thermometer at the same time.*

*The thermometer is an indicator of your strong, usual reaction to this person. When the liquid in the thermometer rises, you are responding strongly to this person, becoming judgmental, angry and non-neutral. When the liquid in the thermometer is down, you are neutral, and able to observe this person clearly. Let the liquid in the thermometer be red, or another vivid color.*

*Spend a few moments viewing this person and keeping the thermometer down. Notice what you have to do in order to stop yourself judging and reacting strongly to this person.*

*When you are able, allow yourself to respond more*

*fully to this person, still remaining neutral in the way you react.*

*Why does this person make you uncomfortable? What is it that you would like to communicate to this person?*

*Let your self communicate those things to them. Watch your thermometer. Can you communicate this to them without allowing the liquid in the thermometer to rise? Can you remain in a state of neutrality and still communicate with them?*

*Who do they remind you of? What memories do they trigger?*

*Now observe them neutrally and ask yourself, "What are they trying to communicate to me? Why is it difficult for them?"*

*Ask yourself, "How do they see me?"*

*Now, thank the person for doing this exercise with you.*

*Let their image fade away.*

*Let the glass fade away.*

*Become aware of your breathing. Reflect on what you have learned about yourself, about this person, and about your ability to stay neutral.*

*When you are ready, open your eyes and record the results of this exercise in your journal.*

\* \* \* \* \*

On occasion, in my classes, someone will not be able to get neutral toward the person they choose to do this exercise with. They usually realize how angry they are, but cannot seem to get beyond it. If this happens to you, choose someone else to do this exercise with. Choose someone who does not bug you quite as much.

For others, this exercise has provided a revelation. For the first time they could hear what the person was trying to say to them, ineffectual though their style may be.

## Experiences

One woman realized that an employee of hers was looking to her for approval. She held back her approval because no one had ever approved of her, and she had still made it. She saw her employee's need as a weakness. She realized that instead of just withholding approval, she had been unnecessarily harsh in her criticism. When she later gave approval, her employee blossomed and became a devoted, hard-working asset to the company.

Another person had been dating someone, mostly as a companion, to keep him from feeling lonely. He knew that he did not want the relationship to go any deeper, and he assumed she knew this and felt the same. Still, he had grown distant, and he chose her for this exercise.

He found out how angry she was with him for being distant. She did want a deeper relationship, and had assumed that he did too. She couldn't understand his with-drawal from the relationship whenever it began to get close.

He also realized that he did need her company and that he dearly loved her as a friend and did not want to lose her friendship. If he did not pretend to love her in the way she wanted, he was afraid he would lose her. It became clear from this exercise that he needed to talk truthfully to her, let her know how he cared, and give her the chance to make her own decision about the friendship and relationship.

This was not exactly a happy experience, but it was a relief for him to let his truer feelings come to the surface.

**Variation**: You can substitute a situation for the other person you are in relationship with. For example, many of my students do this exercise with career, job, business, or family to get a new perspective on their relationship with a situation in their life.

Be sure to record your experiences in your journal.

**DAY SEVEN:** Take a few moments to reflect on your life: what you want to experience, what you have experienced, how willing you are to go after what you want, and how limited or unlimited you feel by your circumstances. Ask your Intuition how you can achieve what you want. Be open to the risks involved, emotionally as well as physically and financially. Write your thoughts and results in your journal.

* * * * *

## Intuition and Attitude

By now, it is becoming clear that listening to Intuition requires and promotes a certain attitude about life. Listening to Intuition implies taking an active part in our lives. Instead of feeling passive and put upon – victimized by life – Intuition encourages us to be responsible and active in our own lives.

As we become open to the possibilities, we become less restricted by the "normal" and "usual" ways of doing things. Listening to our Intuition implies that we live life "our" way. This does not mean we are opposed to or against anyone else. It just means we discover "our" personal, creative, Intuitive way. It is the way successful people live their lives. I have never heard of a successful person who lived their life "by the book," who did everything just the way they were supposed to do.

## "By the Book" vs. Intuition

This doesn't mean breaking the law, or having to cheat at something. It does mean following the risk-takers, the people who break through stereotypes that dictate what they may and may not do. If there is anybody out there who feels that they have lived their life "by the book" and it has been wonderfully successful for them, I would like to hear from them. Please write to my publisher and let me know.

I have made a personal study of successful individuals. By successful I do not just mean financially. I mean people who are fully satisfied with their lives – which may or may not mean financial success.

It is certainly true that people who want to increase their sensitivity to Intuition tend to be more independent, creative thinkers. A number of studies have shown a correlation between use of Intuition and business success.

Dr. Weston H. Agor has developed a test which evaluates present management styles, intuitive potential (which managers may or may not be aware of), and indicates their management type. In his book, <u>Intuitive Management</u>, he states, "Intuition appears to be a skill that is more prevalent as one moves up the management ladder. Top managers in *every* sample group tested scored higher than middle or lower managers in their *underlying ability* to use intuition to make decisions."

CHAPTER

# 8

## -WEEK SEVEN-
## Applying Your Intuition

*The final act of business judgment is intuitive.*
*— Alfred P. Sloan*

This week we are going to strengthen the relationship to our Intuition even more. My goal for you this week is to develop a sure-fire way to sense an intuitive impression about any situation in your life.

To do this we need to establish an immediate intuitive response that you can not misinterpret or ignore. We are going to bypass all normal analytic thinking processes, and go straight to where our impulses are automatic. I will explain three different ways to establish this. I invite you to try all three, and then use the one that seems to feel most comfortable to you.

\* \* \* \* \*

## EXERCISE ONE:
## THE LIGHTS

**DAY ONE:**

What is your automatic response to a red traffic light?
What is your automatic response to a yellow traffic light?
What is your automatic response to a green traffic light?

Even children who do not drive have learned to automatically stop on red, wait on yellow, and go on green. There is no thinking involved. It is purely automatic.

In our training program for Intuition, we can make great use of this automatic response. We can imagine a traffic light in our minds, and consult it concerning *any* situation. How to proceed? Red, Yellow or Green. Red always means to stop. Go no further. Reevaluate the entire situation before proceeding. Extreme caution.

Yellow always means to wait. Be patient. If you proceed, proceed cautiously. Slow down. Take another look at all aspects of the situation before proceeding.

Green always means keep going. Everything is fine. Continue in the same manner. Go, move, continue action, or take action.

### WARM-UP EXERCISE:

Take a few moments to reflect on a past, successful accomplishment in your life. See if you can remember where you needed to sense a green light in order to keep going. What kept you going? Were there times when you experienced a yellow light? Did you slow down, reevaluate, change direction at all? How do you remember deciding how and when to proceed?

Write these memories in your journal.

* * * * *

Now of course you did not see an actual light at that time. Nor will you necessarily see a light now, even though you know this trick. The lights are there simply to help you clarify and define vague intuitive sensations. You may be involved in some project, or beginning a new relationship, when you suddenly realize *you are feeling uncomfortable.*

Remembering the lights can help you define the feeling. You might ask yourself, "Is this feeling a green light, a red light or a yellow light?" You will instantly be able to characterize your vague feeling, and proceed accordingly.

I remember when my husband and I were thinking of buying our home. We were not sure whether we would be able to afford it. Whenever we would think about whether we should proceed or not, we consulted the lights.

Even during the most discouraging times, the light was always green. We kept on going, and, sure enough, things worked out. My uncomfortable feeling was my own insecurity. My intuition knew that it was the right thing to do and that somehow, things would work out.

\* \* \* \* \*

Now, think of an event that was not successful, a situation in which, in your mind, you failed. Go over the events in your mind. Write them down. Was there a yellow light that you refused to see? Did you ignore a nagging feeling in your own body? When did the red light appear? At what point did you know that it was time to stop? Dead end? What can you learn from reviewing this event? Write all your thoughts in your journal.

**MAIN EXERCISE:**

Imagine a traffic light in your peripheral vision. Place the traffic light on one side of your field of vision; do not let it be in the middle. Make sure that you can sense it clearly. Think of a current situation you are involved in. Check the lights. Which light is on? Reflect on what the light is telling you.

Try another situation. And another.

Spend at least two days working with the traffic lights, and test every situation with them, even the situations in which you already know how to proceed.

**TEST:** Check your emotions. Are you afraid of a particular situation having a particular light associated with it? Do you become emotionally attached to a certain outcome? If so, repeat the neutrality exercise in chapter six.

One student wrote: "I love the lights. They have made it so much easier for me to listen to my Intuition. The lights make it very simple, and very clear. The only problem I have is with the yellow light. I cannot seem to be comfortable with it. I don't like the yellow light because I hate to wait. I just don't want to see it. Red or Green is perfectly fine, I know where I stand, but with yellow the situation seems so unclear, and I just have to wait."

Using this exercise, the lights brought to the surface her impatience. She discovered where her weakness is and could then take steps to strengthen her patience, or at least learn to live with her impatience, and recognize it as a factor in the situations she was dealing with.

Remember that the lights are there to help you define your intuitive feelings. You may never spontaneously see a light, but you will get the *feeling* associated with the lights. And the lights will help you define that feeling more accurately.

\* \* \* \* \*

## EXERCISE TWO:
## THE SOUND

**DAY THREE to DAY FOUR:** For this exercise we need to go back into our Intuition rooms, and establish a link between a sound and our Intuition. After the exercise, the sound will come to you at any time your Intuition wants to communicate with you, whether you are doing the exercise or not.

*Sit down and make yourself comfortable. Take a few deep breaths. Go to the environment where you met your Intuition. By now this process is becoming very natural, and quick.*

*When you get to the environment, take a look around. Remember the details of this place. Notice if anything has changed. If there is something you would like to change or add, do it now.*

*Invite your Intuition to be here with you. Greet your Intuition.*

*Your Intuition is going to help you establish a link between itself and the receptive state you are in now, and your everyday conscious mind.*

*Remember a situation when things did not go right. What did it feel like? Now, listen. Your Intuition will produce a sound or word.*

*Perhaps the sound is a tone, low, high or medium range. Perhaps the sound is a tune you are familiar with or a familiar phrase. Perhaps it is a noise, like a crash, or thunder. Whatever it is, listen to it. Let the sound become very familiar to you. Soak it in. Let the whole environment resonate with this sound.*

*Let the environment become quiet again.*

*Now, remember a situation which required you to wait and be patient. Remember what that felt like. Let your Intuition produce a sound to go with this feeling. As before, it may be a tone, a tune, a familiar phrase or word, or a noise. Let this sound permeate the environment. Soak it in.*

*Let the environment become quiet again.*

*Now, remember a situation when you needed to keep going, or get going, where continued action or new action was required.*

*Remember what that felt like?*

*Let your Intuition produce a sound or word to link with this feeling. It may be a tone, a tune, or a noise. Soak it in, and let it permeate the environment.*

*Now, to try this exercise out, think of a current situation in your life. Listen to the sound that comes with it. Reflect on what the sound and your Intuition are communicating to you.*

*Let all the sounds go and listen to the quiet again. Thank your Intuition. Take a few deep breaths, and when you are ready, open your eyes. Record your experience in your journal.*

**TEST:** Check your emotions. Are you afraid of a particular situation having a particular sound associated with it? Do you become emotionally attached to a certain outcome? If so, repeat the neutrality exercise in chapter six.

When you use this exercise, you may automatically hear the sound or word, and then you will sense what your Intuition is communicating. Or you may need to close your eyes for a few moments to ask about a certain situation and listen for the sound. However it happens, you have created a link between your Intuition and your conscious mind.

\* \* \* \* \*

### EXERCISE THREE:
### THE SENSINGS

**DAY FIVE and DAY SIX:** This exercise applies the same principles as above, but is oriented toward those with strong visual images.

*Sit down and make yourself comfortable. Take a few deep breaths. Go to the environment where you met your Intuition. By now this process is becoming quite natural, and easy.*

*When you get to the environment, take a look around. Remember the details of this place. Notice if anything has changed. If there is something you would like to change, do it now.*

*Invite your Intuition to be here with you. Greet your Intuition.*

*Your Intuition is going to help you establish a link between its presence in the receptive state you are in now, and your everyday conscious mind.*

*Remember a situation when things did not go right, either a situation you have worked with before in this chapter, or another one. What did it feel like? Your Intuition is going to exaggerate this feeling. Where do you feel it in your body? What does it feel like? Have you ever experienced this feeling before?*

*Soak in this sensation; let it be imprinted in your body.*

*Let it go. See your Intuition back in its usual form.*

*Now, think of a situation in which you had to wait and be patient. What did this feel like to you? Again, let your Intuition exaggerate this feeling. Soak in the physical sensation. Then, let it go.*

*Repeat the exercise with a situation that required you to keep going, take action, or proceed as planned. Thank your Intuition. Open your eyes when you are ready. Record your experience in your journal.*

* * * * *

**TEST:** Check your emotions. Are you afraid of a particular situation having a particular outcome? Do you become emotionally attached to a certain outcome? Repeat the neutrality exercise in chapter six.

## Choosing Intuition

One of these exercises will stick with you, either the traffic lights, the sounds or the sensations. You may not want to follow the advice of your Intuition, but you will at least know that your Intuition is communicating with you.

This is a point that is important enough to emphasize. Several of my students were afraid to listen to their Intuition, because they felt that it would overpower their free choice. They felt that once they listened to their Intuition, they would have to follow it, no matter how scary or uncomfortable it might make them.

This is not true. It is important to always feel that *you* are in charge. **It is *you* that makes the decisions in your life, you that has to live with them, and you that has to be responsible for them.** Your Intuition is a good source of information and insight. It makes an important contribution to any decision or action. But it is not mandatory to follow it!

Intuition will not go away if you decide to follow another path. What Intuition needs is acknowledgement for its contribution to your life. It does not need blind obedience. That would be just as unhealthy as always following someone else's advice, or repeating things the way they have always been done in the past.

Any repetitive pattern can become a trap, including doing only what your Intuition tells you, without taking personal responsibility. After all, what is your Intuition? It is you!

# CHAPTER

# 9

## -WEEK EIGHT-
## Test Your Intuition

*Merely recognizing the existence of intuition is a positive first step. This means having faith in the fact that answers to the toughest problems can leap fully conceived into our awareness — and at the most unpropitious moment, as happened to Archimedes in the bath. But this amorphous, ill-defined instinct known as intuition has to be understood, nurtured, and trusted if it is to be turned into a powerful management tool.*
*—Roy Rowan, The Intuitive Manager*

## Quantifying Intuition

Most people, when talking about Intuition, do not think in terms of testing it. While it is true that Intuition does belong to a personal and subjective part of our life, there are ways to test, practice, improve and quantify the reliability of Intuition.

The first objection of many of the businesses that I have spoken to about Intuition training is that Intuition is too vague to be managed well. Although often the same business people admit that Intuition plays an important role in their personal decision making, there does not seem to be a way to observe it and encourage it in their staff.

I have a plan to solve this problem. It works for individuals, and I encourage you to try it. It also increases the credibility of Intuition in group decision-making.

* * * * *

## PLAN ONE:

For at least one week (the longer the better), keep a written record of all intuitive hunches, flashes, feelings, etc. Actively apply all the exercises you have learned from this book, and any other technique that works for you. Number each one. The following page is an example of how your notebook could look. Be sure to allow room for your results under each entry. Discipline yourself to read over your entries every evening, and write in results as they occur.

At the end of the week, or at the end of whatever time you have chosen for this test, divide the number of correct intuitions by the number of entries to get your percentage of accuracy:

$$\frac{\text{correct Intuitions}}{\text{number of entries}} = \text{percentage of accuracy}$$

For example, if someone writes down 20 Intuitions in one week, and let's say that 15 of those are correct, his or her formula would look like this:

$$\frac{15}{20} = 75\% \text{ accurate Intuitions}$$

Intuition becomes more credible when it is quantifiable. A person measuring their intuitive accuracy might

Journal Entry: January 15, 1980

Situation: My first radio interview in a couple of days. I want to be prepared.

Exercise: Preparing for Future Events

Results: At first, I felt very comfortable, then, all of a sudden, I felt very uncomfortable, cautious, off-guard.

Interpretation: Easy questions in the beginning, difficult questions later on in the interview.

Actual Event: Before we went on the air, I spoke with the interviewer. He was very interested in my work and indicated that the interview would go smoothly. I relaxed. Too much. On the air he asked me difficult questions designed to throw me off-balance. I stumbled and struggled to regain my composure. After a few minutes, I was back on track.

Analysis: Intuition was right! I did not remember, and remain cautious.

say, "You know, I have a hunch that this project is on the wrong track, and I have a 75% accuracy rate on my intuitions. So let's go over everything once more and see if we can find a wrong turn."

Sometimes our intuitions are only partially correct. You can factor these into the formula by considering them as half a point.

## Increase Your Reliability

Keeping track of your intuitions and checking their validity is also a great way to test and increase your reliability. When you go back to your journal, examine what you experienced, and compare it to what actually happened, a wonderful thing happens. You learn what intuitions, signals, and signs are most accurate for you – and increase them.

It is somewhat like watching yourself playing golf or tennis, or making a speech on video. When you see yourself making mistakes, you can correct them much more easily than when someone tells you what you have done incorrectly, and then you try to correct it by yourself. Somehow, the body can do more to correct itself after seeing and re-experiencing the situation from a distance.

The same is true for training Intuition. Remember, Intuition is like a muscle. When we observe our own errors it is easy to correct them. The intuitive muscle learns to correct itself.

## Improve Communication With Your Intuition

Another benefit from this method of testing is that you will become more familiar with how your Intuition communicates to you. When you first start tracking your

115

Intuition, you may see visions or symbols that you do not understand. When you return to them later, after an event has taken place, you may say, "Oh, now I know what that was telling me." Understanding your Intuition takes time and is part of developing good communication.

* * * * *

## PLAN TWO:

There are several questions that you can ask yourself, to check your intuitive information for accuracy. This is an extremely tricky area to get into. Many of us probably question our intuitions too much anyway, and that is how we talk ourselves out of believing them.

You can recognize the questions by their qualities. They tend to put a stop to any more questions; they ridicule and make intuitions look stupid, and they are always critical. I call that kind of questioning "Doubting Questions/ Statements." Doubting Questions tend to undermine your trust of your Intuition and make it look stupid. And the doubts almost always seem like they are coming from someone else. Let's look at those and get them out of the way.

## DOUBTING QUESTIONS/STATEMENTS

1. How could this be true?
2. No one else does it this way, so I can't.
3. This could never happen.
4. No one will believe me. There is no way I can sell this to others.
5. This will only fail.

6. I am making this up.
7. Who do I think I am to try this?
8. This is a stupid idea.

## The Chatterbox

You can see that these statements make it difficult to go on, to explore, to test if there might be a possibility that your Intuition has a good insight. I call the part of our mind that asks these questions "the chatterbox." We all have a part of our mind that is constantly undermining our Intuition. It seems to go on and on.

At first, students try to ignore it and resist it. This approach never works. The chatterbox needs attention, and needs to be acknowledged. I say to my chatterbox, "I hear you, but right now I am listening to my Intuition. You can quiet down now." This way I don't try to fight my chatterbox. Fighting only serves to increase the conflict and take attention away from my Intuition.

## The Doubting Mind

The Doubting Mind creates the chatterbox. Doubting Questions close the door on our Intuition by focusing on fears and ignorance. Instead of looking realistically at what you are afraid of, Doubting Questions assume that fears are insurmountable and that we should stop all further action and investigation.

A useful way to deal with fears is to look at them directly. Let your imagination have full rein to think of your worst fears. Write them down and look at them. Spend time looking at what the worst expectations can bring and how you could respond to those situations.

Managers know this system as "failure analysis." It is a useful tool for getting the fears out of your mind and down on paper. When you look at the worst, you can better determine how it could be solved, and whether or not you are willing to take the risk to proceed.

Edgar Mitchell, the *Apollo 14* astronaut, explains: "With a computer printout of the resulting 'fault tree' [from failure analysis] in front of him, a boss can almost smell those failures before they occur." (That sounds like Intuition to me.) Looking neutrally at a list of possible disasters, your Intuition can pick out the ones to focus on.

## Encourage Your Intuition

There are some questions and statements you can make to your Intuition that can encourage it, help it and test it. It is important to determine if a message from your Intuition is influenced by your fears or your desires or your Expert Mind.

Intuition always comes *from you..* Even if you perceive it through symbols or images, it comes from you and **it feels like you are talking to yourself**. The following statements/questions are a guide to understanding the nature of Intuition and testing the validity of intuitive flashes.

### GUIDING QUESTIONS/STATEMENTS

1. Intuition is neutral and can bring a feeling of fullness with it.
2. Intuition can be a guide for the future and always gives directions for the present.
3. Is my Intuition dependent upon the action,

acknowledgement or approval of anyone else?
4. Does this Intuition feel right?
5. Is there something I can proceed with immediately?
6. Can I recognize the connection between this Intuition and other pertinent information and facts regarding this situation?
7. Is there a possible positive outcome for others and me?
8. Can I recognize and analyze or acknowledge the risks, possible failures and disasters?

This list of questions/statements is just a guide to point you in the right direction. It is not necessary that Intuition answer all of the above questions; only some may be relevant to you. Remember that the questions are to help you determine whether you are getting stuck in your Doubting Mind, and to ask questions that may make the Intuition more practical. Intuitions always leave the door open, never closed. With Intuition, the decision is up to you. Intuition only gives information.

* * * * *

**PLAN THREE:**

This plan details in depth some of the problems mentioned in the other two plans. Fears and desires will interrupt your intuitive process only when they go unchecked. If I am afraid of having my teeth worked on by a dentist, I will ignore, avoid and put off any symptom that may lead to my going to the dentist. My Intuition cannot offer anything to those issues because I won't listen.
Another example of a slightly different form of fear

and desire happened to me this morning when I sat down to write this section. First I went over some chapters to add and delete a few sentences. While I was doing this I had a flash that I should push the "save" button on my computer to make sure what I added would not be erased by a possible electrical outage.

I did not listen to that flash. Perhaps I was too lazy, or more likely, I was too afraid to even consider the possibility that all I had worked on would be lost. It was definitely an intuitive flash, because a few minutes later, my dog walked over to where I was sitting and knocked out the plug. I lost what I had just written and had to do it over anyway.

Try the following plan to explore a current situation in more detail:

1. Write down your situation, plan, program, or question.
2. Make a list of all the possible outcomes of your situation. Put them all down: the positive outcomes you would like to see; the exaggerated, ultimately positive outcomes; the outcomes that produce more problems and go against your desire; and the fearful outcomes – the worst expectations possible. List them all as neutrally and objectively as possible. As you write them down, notice which ones you get excited about and which ones you get very nervous about.
3. Review Doubting Questions and Guiding Questions. Which ones seem to apply to your sense of this situation?
4. Next to each outcome, write how you would possibly respond.
5. Ask your Intuition to give you any further information on each item. Write your intuitive response to each item.

After you experiment with these three plans to test your Intuition, the testing process will happen more quickly. It is important to remember that the purpose of testing Intuition is to increase the strength of your intuitive muscle. Testing helps to fine tune your recognition of intuitive information.

## Impulsive or Intuitive?

One of the most difficult questions I get asked at every class is, "How can I tell the difference between an impulsive feeling and an intuitive knowing?" It is a good question because there are similarities. They can both feel important and compelling. They both feel very "right."

## Impulsive

There are some very subtle and important differences. An impulse always feels like it has to be done immediately; if you wait, you will miss your opportunity. With an impulse, we feel under pressure to act. After we act impulsively, we feel empty. It did not solve the problem. Impulses are, as the word implies, a strong burst of energy followed by quiet. Impulses come on strong, and then fade away.

## Intuitive

An Intuition may be compelling, but there is always time to reflect. I use what I call the Universal Law of Three. If I find something I want to buy – usually clothes are impulsive for me – I try it on and then continue to look elsewhere. I let it go in my mind. If it comes back, I do the same thing again. If it comes back to me again, I buy it. If something comes back to me three times, I do it. Intuitions are consistent and persistent. If it is important, you will not forget it, it will keep coming back to you. It will nag you.

I have several stock brokers as students. In their business they have to act quickly. But even under intense pressure, they can use the Law of Three. Within a few moments they can let an idea go, and wait. If it comes back right away, let it go again, and wait. They have learned to sense the difference between a panic reaction and an Intuition. Their Intuitions usually come just before a change in the stock market. A panic happens after a change has already occurred.

## Impulsive:

- compelling
- immediate
- no time to think
- a feeling of desperate need

## Intuitive:

- consistent
- persistent
- immediacy not as important
- use the Law of Three

CHAPTER

# 10

## -WEEK NINE-
## Making Intuition
## A Part Of Your Life

*This 'gift' [Intuition] was long considered to be the property of gods or spirits, not the heritage of ordinary men and women. Few people considered the possibility that such sporadic instances of intuition might be lower-order manifestations of a capacity that could be developed until it became a reliable channel of knowing.*
—*Arthur J. Deikman, M.D., from* The Observing Self

### Unexpected Intuition

There are two ways to receive intuitive information. One way I call the **Maintenance Program**. It is similar to physical exercise that you do to keep yourself in good shape, generally. The Maintenance Program for Intuition keeps your mind open to intuitive impressions that can come at any time, any place, concerning any situation.

This is the Intuition most people are familiar with. At

any time, when you least expect it, a flash of insight can occur. In the past this type of Intuition was treated as a goddess. People prayed to her, and waited for her to bless them with her knowledge and insight. To talk to her or about her too much would ruin the magic.

With a Maintenance Program, a part of your mind remains attuned to intuitive impressions and passes them on to your conscious mind for evaluation. It is an exercise program that keeps the channel open.

I believe that most of us have many, many intuitive flashes that pass us by because we have not trained ourselves to notice them. They can be easily dismissed. They are barely recognized by a mind that is not trained to welcome them.

Your Maintenance Program will strengthen the link between your Intuition and your conscious mind so that messages can travel easily between them. Your particular Maintenance Program is based on your needs and situation.

## Accessing Intuition On Demand

The other way we receive intuitive information is through what I call **Direct Access**.

Direct Access is when we ask our Intuition for specific information about a specific situation. Many of the exercises in this book are Direct Access exercises and you can invent many more to suit the particular situation you are in.

With Direct Access exercises, you don't need to wait for the Goddess of Intuition to bless you with her insights. You can ask her what you need to know directly, and receive an answer. The Direct Access program gives you control over your Intuition. It is analogous to the physical exercises you would do to strengthen a particular part of your body.

## Categories for Intuition Workout Exercises

### Maintenance Exercises:
MEET YOUR INTUITION (Ch. 2)
RELEASING FEARS* (Ch. 4)
UNDERSTANDING DESIRE* (Ch. 5)
THE BUBBLE (Ch. 6)
RELEASING PAST AND FUTURE (Ch. 7)
PRACTICING NEUTRALITY (Ch. 7)

*These can also be used as Direct Access exercises when we have a very *specific* fear or desire we want to understand, although generally speaking it is useful to examine our fears and desires on a regular basis.

### Direct Access Exercises:
ASK YOUR INTUITION A QUESTION (Ch. 2)
DECISION PATHS (Ch. 3)
SENSING BODY INTUITION (Ch. 3)
PREPARING FOR FUTURE EVENTS (Ch. 3)
BUBBLE, WITH A SPECIFIC SITUATION (Ch. 6)

As you can see, **Maintenance Exercises** develop a *general awareness and understanding* of how our Intuition works. The **Direct Access** exercises apply Intuition to *specific situations*. You can make up an exercise to fit a particular situation if none of the above can be applied to your situation.

125

* * * * *

# Developing Your Unique Program

**TIME AND PLACE:** At least one Maintenance Exercise needs to be done each day. Ideally, there should be a specific time of each day set aside to stay in touch with your Intuition. The right time of day for you is a decision you need to make. For some of my students the morning is the best time because that is when they feel most alert.

For others, the morning is too hectic to take a few moments out, and just before lunch, or just after lunch is a much better time. Some students prefer their exercise time at home, while for others the office is better. Others do their exercises while commuting on the train or bus. You need to make a decision about the best time and place for you. You may even want to consult your Intuition about this.

The most important component in your Maintenance Program is consistency. If you can only do your exercises three times a week, then that is OK, as long as you **do** it three times a week. After you get comfortable with your Maintenance Program you may not even need to sit down, close your eyes, and play music. When I have a very busy day ahead of me, I do my exercises in the shower.

## Sample Maintenance Plans

Six Day A Week Plan: (For the ambitious and enthusiastic):
**DAY ONE:** MEET YOUR INTUITION and Direct Access Exercise of choice;
**DAY TWO:** RELEASING FEARS and Direct Access

Exercise of choice;

**DAY THREE:** MEET YOUR INTUITION and Direct Access Exercise of choice;

**DAY FOUR:** UNDERSTANDING DESIRE and Direct Access Exercise of choice;

**DAY FIVE:** MEET YOUR INTUITION and Direct Access Exercise of choice;

**DAY SIX:** RELEASING PAST AND FUTURE and Direct Access Exercise of choice.

If you want to do an exercise every day, but do not have the time to do both, alternate between a Maintenance Exercise and a Direct Access Exercise.

* * * * *

Four Day Per Week Plan: (days need not be consecutive):

**DAY ONE:** MEET YOUR INTUITION and Direct Access Exercise of your choice;

**DAY TWO AND THREE:** Choose one Maintenance Exercise other than MEET YOUR INTUITION, and Direct Access Exercise of your choice;

**DAY FOUR:** MEET YOUR INTUITION and Direct Access Exercise of your choice.

* * * * *

Two Day Per Week Plan:

**DAY ONE:** MEET YOUR INTUITION and Direct Access Exercise of your choice;

**DAY TWO:** Maintenance Exercise of your choice, and Direct Access Exercise of your choice.

* * * * *

127

By this time you can use your Intuition to help you determine what program will be the best for you, or make up your own. The most important thing is to DO IT! Like any other skill, the more you practice, the more reliable your Intuition will be.

Use the next page in your journal to develop your own plan.

CHAPTER

# 11

# -WEEK TEN-
# Synchronicity and Group Exercises

*...stars cannot be seen in midday, yet are there nonetheless.*
  *—Jean Bolen, M.D. The Tao Of Psychology*

Before you read the next two chapters, you may want to feel comfortable with the rest of the book first. In this chapter I will be discussing advanced techniques for training and using your Intuition. When I teach a beginning class, I use some of these techniques to stretch the intuitive muscle of the participants far beyond what they imagine they could do, in order to inspire them.

Much more is possible in a guided group than with an individual working alone. I can't explain why, but I know from experience that the energy generated by a group inspires each individual to go beyond what they would do alone. Perhaps it is similar to performing. The excitement of an audience can stimulate the skilled performer to act with a creative touch not present in rehearsal.

Most of the exercises in this chapter require at least two people and preferably more to get the full effect.

The first area we will consider is Synchronicity. In the beginning of this book I mentioned that "experience" was also a form of communication used by our Intuition. Synchonicity is what I was referring to. An external experience, meaning something that happens *to us*, can be a form of intuitive knowing.

## Synchronicity

I define synchronicity as **an external event which triggers an internal knowing**. It has to do with events that are significant coincidences, such as when you are trying to solve a problem and someone "just happens" to call. During the conversation the caller "just happens" to give a clue or answer to the difficulty.

A woman in one of my classes told me a story that illustrates synchonicity. She had been in a depression for several months; she was away from home, and for the previous year she had continually been ill.

One day, while riding in a taxi through Times Square in New York City, she saw a movie theater with two shows playing. One was "Death Wish" and the one underneath it on the marquee was "Sharon" – her name. This triggered her into realizing that she was pulling herself down. The experience motivated her to decide to go on with her life, and develop a more positive attitude. That was a meaningful moment of synchronicity.

Another person told the story of the time she went to interview for a new job. As she walked into the waiting room, she noticed that the art on the wall was by an artist she happened to admire. At that point she knew that the job was hers. It didn't matter that she did not get the job on the first interview. She felt certain of it, and sure enough, she got the job. It has been a place where she enjoys working.

Is this magic?

No. It is another form of Intuition. Sometimes our intuitive mind uses an *external* stimulation to jolt us into recognizing an *inner* knowing. It is important to realize that the inner knowing is the most important part.

## Synchronicity Not Superstition

If there is no inner knowing, there is no synchronicity. In other words, if someone tries to find or analyze the meaning of an event, it is not synchronicity. It can turn into superstition. If I try to figure out what it means when the car doesn't start, or the weather is bad, or when I forget my keys, it is not synchronicity. I am just trying to make something more meaningful than it is.

Reading meanings into external events can be comforting, as we then allow the event to give us direction, rather than thinking and deciding for ourselves. The trick to recognizing synchronicity is to realize that the inner knowing takes place *immediately*.

Another student of mine told the story of a time when she was working quickly Friday afternoon because she wanted to get to a store before it closed. In her haste, she "accidentally" locked her purse in her bottom drawer, one with an automatic lock. The key was...in her purse!

She knew at that moment that she would not get to the store on time. So, she decided to relax and stay later to complete some projects she was working on. Her Intuition used that event to trigger her inner knowing about the work that needed to be done in a quiet space.

131

Every time someone locks their keys somewhere does not guarantee a synchronistic experience! The *event* was unimportant compared to the *inner knowing* that went with it. The inner knowing is personal, and unique for the situation and the person.

## Triggering Synchronicity

Synchronicity usually just happens, but there are some tricks you can use to induce it. Remember, throughout all these techniques, that **the power is in you, not in the technique.** The purpose of the technique is merely to stimulate an inner knowing. Sometimes it will happen and sometimes it will not. You are the only one who can determine if you have a synchronistic experience.

## You Can't Make Deals With Synchronicity

Sometimes we want so much for someone or something to tell us what to do, that we try and make a deal with synchronicity. For example, we might say, "If the light is green at the next street corner, I will go to the party on Saturday."

When we formulate an "if...then" statement with two unrelated items, we are trying to make a deal with synchronicity. This is just like reading meaning into something which is not inherently there. It is another form of superstition.

Every superstition begins with a synchronistic experience. It is usually unique to one person or one group of people. It becomes a tradition because of the importance of the original synchronistic event. Over time, the inner meaning is usually lost.

There are superstitions which maintain that walking under a ladder, or breaking a mirror, brings bad luck. Somewhere, sometime, an unfortunate event may have followed these actions. But to continue to breathe life into those traditions is superstition, not Intuition. Every culture has superstitions. To which ones do you still pay service? What are you afraid will happen if you disobey the superstition? Usually these fears are nameless, and therefore can't be easily examined. If you have alot of superstitions and are tired of having them run your life, go back to the chapter on fear and use the Main Exercise in that week, substituting superstitions for fears.

* * * * *

## SYNCHRONICITY GAMES:

The following exercises are called "games" because that is the best attitude to have when triggering a synchronistic experience. If you are "working," or trying too hard, you will not be open to an inner knowing. So relax, and have fun with your Intuition!

**CONSULT AN ORACLE:** All oracles can produce synchronicity. Their accuracy relies on the inner knowing of the person consulting them. Some of the ones I have found useful are the I Ching, Tarot Cards, Runes, Angel Cards, The Bible, a good friend, a counselor, and many others.

The oracle is a synchronistic experience because you are asking a question and leaving it up to what transpires in that present moment to trigger a greater understanding in you. If the oracle triggers an internal knowing in you, then it has worked. If not, then the oracle has not worked that time.

It is important to remember that the power is not in the oracle but in the person using the oracle. You are the one who understands what the oracle is saying to you and what its meaning is.

**FLIP A COIN:** When you have a decision to make and you just can't decide which way to go, flip a coin. Whether the coin is heads or tails does not matter, what matters is how you feel when the coin comes up heads or tails. Did it come out the way you wanted? Now you know more about what you want.

**GROUP SYNCHRONICITY GAME:** When I teach a class, I usually do this game near the end. You need at least three people. Each person thinks of something in their life that they would like to know the answer to. It could be a problem, situation or decision. Each person phrases this unknown to themselves so that it can be answered with either "yes" or "no."

Each person takes two pieces of paper and writes "yes" on one and "no" on the other. Each piece of paper is folded at least two times so that no one can see which paper has which word. Each person stands up and mixes up the pieces of paper. Then everyone begins to trade papers with everyone else. They keep trading for several minutes to make sure that they trade both pieces of paper several times. If they happen to end up with one of their own, that's OK.

Now, each person opens the paper they ended with and waits for an inner knowing. Did they get what they expected? Not what they expected? The important thing is how they feel about the word on the paper.

The words on the papers have no power over the future. They are just to jolt a synchronistic experience. It's really fun to do with a large group.

As long as we are talking about a large group, I want to share another exercise I conduct with a group of people to stretch their intuitive muscle.

This exercise is impossible. There is really no way that what I am about explain to you will make any sense. Just humor me. Go along because you have been going along for the rest of the book, even though you will soon see that there is no way that you or anybody you know could perform the next task. All you can do is do it and not try, because no amount of trying will help.

**GROUP EXERCISE ONE:** Everyone in the group gets a piece of paper. Everyone in the group writes a question concerning a current problem, decision or situation that they would like some advice on. Be as simple and concise as possible.

When everyone has finished writing, fold the pieces of paper a couple of times so that the writing does not show. Then the leader of the group collects the papers, mixes them up, and hands them out to the group randomly. Now, everyone is holding a folded piece of paper with someone else's, (perhaps their own, we don't know) problem written on the inside where they cannot see it.

So far this has been easy. Now comes the impossible part. I guide each of the people in the group to tune in to what is on the piece of paper *and* what the solution is *without allowing them to look at the piece of paper*. I know this is impossible, which is why I do it.

Strangely enough, in all of my groups, after their intuitive muscles have been warmed up, there is an 80-90% accuracy rate. The participants may not get the exact wording on the paper, although sometimes some words are the same, but they do get the feeling, or the image, or the sense of what the problem is. Most of the time, within the images or symbols imagined is the solution.

* * * * *

You may be wondering what this exercise really has to do with Intuition. And when would you ever be able to apply this exercise to the real world anyway?

## The Infinite Mind and the Real World

For one thing, the exercise stretches your intuitive muscle way beyond what you thought possible, so confidence and strength increase. It is a wonderful feeling when you find out how your imaginings apply to another person. Participants are truly amazed at themselves, and have a greater sense of where their intuitive muscle is, and how it works.

We could talk about Intuition for the next twenty years and you would still not know how to use it or what it felt like when you did. After an exercise like this, you know much more clearly where **your** intuitive muscle is and how it functions.

As to the question of the real world, there have been occasions where I have used this exercise in real-life situations. In a corporate office, or board meeting, where the members have acknowledged the value of their Intuition, they may be guided through this exercise to consider important questions and decisions.

This exercise truly bypasses the Expert Mind. How can you possibly think about what the right solution is when you don't even know the question? The insights gained from this exercise can give a whole new perspective on any situation. A new perspective is valuable within any decision-making process.

* * * * *

**GROUP EXERCISE TWO:** Any nonverbal process can be a valuable tool for accessing your Intuition. Techniques I often use in my workshops include drawing, coloring and painting. Somehow, through drawing, participants reveal to themselves and others their deeper feelings and thoughts about a situation.

Through drawing, the feelings and insights that our conscious mind filters (and perhaps judges as unacceptable) come through. Sometimes I have participants switch to their non-dominant hand while drawing. This usually allows even deeper feelings and thoughts to emerge.

To structure the drawings, I ask participants either to draw a picture of the situation or decision they are contemplating, or simply draw anything that occurs to them after we have completed one of the visualization exercises (The Paths, Future Events, etc.). With something to focus on, the drawings can begin, and the rest just comes out. For example, one person was thinking about his business partner and started drawing a flower. The flower was a large sunflower, tall and strong. When we talked about he flower, he realized that it had very shallow roots and was top heavy. (Not all sunflowers are like this, but his was.) At first this alarmed him. He thought the shallow roots depicted his partner's long term intentions. However, on further reflection and communication with his partner, he realized that he, himself, was the deeply rooted and grounded person in their relationship. He took care of details, while his partner expanded the business with vision. They needed each other.

It is important to remember that this is a fun exercise. Even if people have never drawn a picture, or think that they cannot do anything right or well, this exercise takes them back to being a child – having fun, playing – and their expression comes through naturally.

**EXERCISE THREE:** Pick an exercise that you enjoyed from the book, and repeat it. Then draw a picture based on your feelings, images, and sensings.

# CHAPTER

# 12

## -WEEK ELEVEN-
## Health, Money and Relationships

*A moment's experience is something worth a life's experience.*

*— Oliver W. Holmes*

There are a few questions concerning the use of Intuition that people ask frequently:

Can Intuition let me know when my health is failing?

Can Intuition help me make the right financial moves?

I keep falling in love with the wrong person. Can Intuition help me choose the right person?

These issues are important to all of us. The answer to all of these questions is: "yes," "no," and "maybe." As you probably know by now, the issues of relationships, health and money are packed with emotions, desires, fears and expectations. You have probably used one of these areas in the other exercises in this book.

Intuition plays a large role in these three major areas of anyone's life. But they are full of emotional obstacles. These obstacles hinder the use of Intuition when any of these areas are involved, so it is worth spending some extra time on them.

## Jumping the Hurdles

Our involvements with health, money and relationships usually bring our fears, desires and expectations to the forefront. These things are precisely what **get in the way** of our ability to listen to our Intuition!

If we can clear a pathway through these obstacles, the answer is, "Yes, Intuition can help us." If they get in the way a little bit, the answer is, "Maybe." If we can recognize what gets in our way and deal with that, then Intuition can help us.

If the obstacles are greater than our ability to get through them right now, the answer is, "No, we cannot trust our impulses." Perhaps we need professional guidance in sorting out the obstacles first.

There are a few tricks that may help you sort through some of the obstacles to get down to what your Intuition is trying to communicate to you.

## Intuition and Health

The following exercise is designed to help you prevent disease and possibly, in some cases, recognize that your body needs professional help. Good health is important for everyone. Americans spend billions of dollars on health plans, clubs, fad diets, vitamins, exercise classes and health evaluations. How often does someone ask Intuition about what their body needs?

For some people this is a simple and wonderful exercise. For others it is a bit more difficult to get through fears and desires and Expert Mind. For those who think they know what their bodies need, Expert Mind will get in the way. You may need to review the necessary exercises. In any case, this exercise should relax and refresh you.

**This exercise is not intended to replace any medical examinations or health and fitness evaluations you may require.** It is intended to enhance those examinations and give you a sense of what your body needs so you can discuss it with the professional(s) of your choice.

*  *  *  *  *

### WELLNESS EXERCISE

*Sit down and make yourself comfortable. Close your eyes. Take a few deep breaths. While you are breathing, imagine that the air around you is filled with sparkling bits of golden energy. As you continue to breathe, you breathe in the energy.*

*This golden energy represents the life force, vitality, and wellness. This golden energy gently dissolves any tension, any discomfort, any distraction. These things release with every exhalation. Feel yourself inhaling the sparkling fragments of golden energy, and let them refresh you.*

*Now you can begin to direct the sparkling bits of golden energy to make sure they reach every part of you. First, direct the energy to your feet. Feel the sparkling bits of golden energy flowing down your legs and into your feet. Feel the sparkling energy circulating through your toes, over the soles of your feet and up your ankles. Remember to exhale all the tension, discomfort and dis-*

141

tractions with every exhalation, and let the sparkling fragments of energy refresh and revive you.

Now, let the sparkling energy fill up your legs. Like a glass of water filling up, let the sparkling energy fill up your legs. Feel it getting into every crack and crevice. Then let your torso fill up with the sparkling bits of golden energy.

Make sure every part is touched and soothed, energized and refreshed by the sparkling bits of golden energy.

*Let yourself enjoy the feeling of letting go of tension, of letting in refreshment, as the sparkling bits of golden energy fill up your ribs and chest, upper back and shoulders. Feel the sparkling energy overflowing and pouring into your arms, around your elbows and into your hands. Feel the sparkles circulating around your fingers and thumbs.*

*Go up into your neck, and feel the sparkles filling up your neck, going up into your jaw and up through your face and head. Feel the sparkles permeate your ears, cheeks nose and eyes. It even fills your eyelids and eyelashes. Each place the sparkles find, they release and relax and energize.*

*Let the point between your eyebrows be filled with the sparkles and feel them filling up to the top of your head. Imagine the sparkles going into your scalp and hair. You are now completely relaxed, and refreshed at the same time. The sparkling bits of golden energy are continuing to permeate you, gently dissolving all tension, discomfort, distractions and disturbing thoughts, and releasing them with every exhalation.*

*Now, go into the environment you created, where you met your Intuition. As you feel yourself there, notice if anything has changed, if there is anything you would like to change. Make yourself comfortable.*

*Next door, or near this place, you are going to create a new place. The new place is going to be your ideal healing environment. Imagine yourself walking over to the new place, or walking through the door that leads to your healing environment.*

*When you get there, look around. What kind of place is this? What kinds of objects, toys, equipment, etc. are*

143

*there? Is color important here? Is decoration and ambience important here? How does the air feel? Be sure to make yourself as comfortable as possible here.*

*This is a place to heal. It is the ideal environment for your body, mind and spirit to come together for the purpose of healing. Whatever you want here you can have. Whatever makes you comfortable you can create.*

*Now invite in your ideal physician. Someone who you trust completely with your body, mind and spirit. Someone who knows everything about you and who knows everything about healing.*

*Whoever this is, let him or her in. It may be someone you know, but even more perfect. Your choice may be a fantasy of someone you have heard about but have not met. It may be a complete surprise, or it may feel obvious, and the only choice for you. Whoever it is does not matter. What matters is that the person knows you, and you trust them completely.*

*Let your physician give you a complete examination. Someone this sensitive to you may just need to look at you to know exactly what is going on in your body. Or perhaps a more conventional examination takes place. Perhaps some equipment is used in the examination.*

*As the examination is taking place, and afterwards, listen to what your physician discovers about you. Listen to what you physician recommends for you. And if there is some healing that can take place now, let it happen. Let your physician perform any healing in any form that can take place right now.*

*Listen to what your physician tells you about what you need to do to improve your health and vitality.*

*Thank your physician for coming to see you. Let your*

*physician leave this healing place.*

*Go back into your main room where you met your Intuition. Take a few moments to feel and enjoy the healing that has taken place. Now gently bring yourself back into the chair you are sitting in. Remember the sparkling bits of golden energy that are still swirling through your body. Enjoy them too.*

*Breathe deeply, breathe deeply again. Gently bring your awareness into your body, into the chair you are sitting in, and when you are ready, open your eyes.*

*Record all events in your journal.*

* * * * *

## Experiences

This exercise has produced amazing and varied results. Physicians seen in this exercise have ranged from Dr. Kildare to a shaman doctor from a Native American tribe. Physicians have been women, men and children. Religious figures such as Jesus Christ and the Virgin Mary have appeared as healing physicians.

My doctor is an ancient Chinese physician who uses pulse diagnosis to determine my state of health. Now in real life, I do not have an ancient Chinese doctor, but in my meditation that is who appeared, and I trust his judgment. He seems to know everything about the body, the mind and the emotions.

Other students of mine have had doctors who use herbs, vitamins and massage. Others have had psychic surgeons tell them what to watch out for. Anything is possible in our imagination; there are absolutely no limits.

If you felt that you were too afraid to listen to your doctor, or felt that you were hearing just what you wanted to hear, or perhaps you didn't learn anything about yourself that you didn't already know, there are exercises that can help open your mind. Go back to the exercises in previous chapters that relate to your particular situation.

If you felt afraid, do the Releasing Fear Exercise. If you were hearing what you wanted to hear, do the Desire Exercise. If you were hearing only what you already know, go back to Beginners Mind.

Sometimes you may have the feeling that you already knew what the doctor was telling you, but you had been ignoring it, or hadn't paid much attention. This can be a valid form of Intuition, letting you know that what you *do* know is important and needs to be taken seriously. Every Intuition is not a revelation. Sometimes our Intuition is right in line with what we know. That's great. Keep up the good work.

For the next two advanced topics, relationships and money, we combine some of the techniques we have already learned, and direct them specifically to the sensitive areas.

## Money and Intuition

One of the very first things that people ask when they hear about the kind of work I do is, "Can you apply your Intuition to stock market trends and investments?"

Money comes under the heading of a highly charged emotional issue. Most of us have many layers of learned attitudes about money, conscious and unconscious, that control our financial success one way or the other. These usually interfere with our ability to listen to our Intuition on money issues.

The following exercises will hopefully clarify your

Intuition on money matters. They are a combination of techniques you have already practiced, specifically applied to money.

But first ask yourself the questions below. There are no right or wrong answers. These questions are designed to stimulate your thoughts and feelings about money. Write down your honest answers and reflect on how your attitude about money determines the relationship you have with money now in your life.

## Money Questions

Is money good or bad?

If I had all the money I wanted, what would I do? How would money change my life?

What does the amount of money I have in my life now keep me from doing? Or, what does it motivate me to do?

What is (was) my parents' attitude about money? Is mine the same?

How has money determined my life?

How would I feel if tomorrow, all my money was gone?

Now we can go on to explore the relationship with money even further.

* * * * *

### MONEY EXERCISE

*Sit down and make yourself comfortable. Close your eyes. Take a few deep breaths. While you are breathing, imagine that the air around you is filled with sparkling bits of golden energy. As you continue to breathe, breathe in*

147

the sparkling bits of golden energy.

This golden energy represents the life force, vitality, and wellness. This golden energy gently dissolves any tension, any discomfort, any distraction. Feel them release with every exhalation. Feel yourself inhaling the sparkling bits of golden energy, and let them refresh you. With every exhalation, let go of all your tension, discomfort and distractions.

Now direct the sparkling bits of golden energy to make sure they reach every part of you, as you did in the health exercise. If you did not do the wellness exercise, just relax and breathe the sparkling bits of golden energy in deeply. Let the energy circulate through all parts of your body. Let your exhalations release all tensions, distractions and discomforts.

Take a few moments to think about money. Let an image form in your mind that represents money to you. Take your time. There is no need to force anything here. We all have a relationship with money, and the most appropriate image and symbol will appear automatically.

Place the image that symbolizes money to you above the top of your head. Take a few moments to feel it there. Does it have weight? Does it take up space? How does it feel up there?

Now, let a piece of this symbol break off and drop into your body. Just open up and let the piece of this symbol fall into you. It will land somewhere; there will be some-place where the symbol lands and feels stuck or lodged.

Perhaps it will lodge in more than one place. That is fine. See if you can notice where it first lodged, or where it seems heaviest. Now, let your awareness go to that place where it is heaviest, or where the symbol is lodged. Take a

HARMON

*few moments to sense how it feels, how it would look if you could see it, and what texture(s) and color(s) it has.*

*Ask the following questions and wait for an answer. If no answer occurs, just go on to the next question.*

*Are there any memories associated with this feeling?*

*If this feeling could talk, what would it say to me?*

*How does this feeling affect my attitude and relationship with money? Is it supportive? Does it interfere?*

*Think of an important current situation involving money. How would this feeling approach and deal with this issue which is in my life right now?*

*If this feeling were not in my life, how would I approach this situation?*

*Say thank you for any and all of the information you have received. Release the feeling in your body and let the image above your head gently dissolve.*

*Feel yourself breathing deeply, and gently bring yourself back into your chair. When you are ready you can open your eyes. Record your experience in your journal .*

* * * * *

## Experiences

As you can see, this exercise makes specific use of the Intuition exercise we did in the second chapter of this book. Some people find that the piece of money that gets lodged in their body is helpful to their relationship with money. Others realize that certain attitudes they are carrying around are detrimental to their relationship with money. In this exercise you can explore your unconscious feelings about money.

150

One person had the dollar symbol, $, as their symbol for money (not as common as you might think). The piece that broke off landed in her head, in about the center. It represented the feeling she had that she **deserved** money.

She went further, to associate her habit of spending more money than she had to with this feeling. Living within her means somehow meant that she wasn't getting what she deserved. She had recently gotten tired of being in debt and this exercise helped her break through the emotional barrier to living within her means.

Another student felt the piece of money near the small of his back. He discovered from the feeling that money was a burden that kept him from doing what he really wanted to do.

Going a little deeper, he realized that money became associated with the fear of doing what he really wanted to do. In other words, his reasoning was that if he did what he wanted to do, there would be no money. Needing to make money kept him from even thinking about what he really wanted to do.

This recognition helped him to evaluate what he really wanted to do in terms of the money it might produce. He found out that it would generate money if he structured it appropriately.

For someone else, the symbol for money was a gold key. The key represented power, and it dropped into his stomach area. For him, money represented power, the power to do what he wanted; the power to control situations in his life.

Going deeper, he discovered that many times in business situations he felt out of control and at the mercy of the other people involved. Consequently, he had trouble asking for the amount of money he deserved, and he felt a loss of power.

Understanding the relationship between the two, he concentrated on recognizing the value he brought to his business dealings. He began to value himself more.

## More Money Exercises

The following exercises can be useful in exploring financial situations and decisions, as well as clearing away the fears and desires that get in the way of Intuition. By now you can determine for yourself which exercises are appropriate for your situation.

> DECISION PATHS
> RELEASING FEARS
> UNDERSTANDING DESIRE
> PREPARING FOR FUTURE EVENTS

## Intuition and Relationships

For most of us, relationships are both a wonderful and difficult area. Sometimes we find ourselves in a relationship where we are wondering how to get closer. Other times we wonder whether we are really getting what we need from our partnerships.

Knowing whether to work it through or move on is always a difficult decision. Sometimes we wonder how to communicate more clearly with someone, or perhaps we find ourselves drifting and avoiding real contact with someone we love.

## What Gets In the Way?

Directing our Intuition to relationships can be a tricky and treacherous area. Our emotional needs, desires and fears will constantly get in the way. Our Expert Mind, coming from years of dictating what should be good for us, can also get in the way of our inner knowing.

The first thing we need to do is to practice neutrality. As difficult as it may sound in some situations, it is a key to clearly seeing and knowing what is going on in a relationship, and how to proceed.

## Neutrality in Relationships and Intuition

A little neutrality can go a long way toward letting yourself grow within a relationship. It can help you listen more carefully to what someone might be trying to communicate to you. It can help you know what it is you are trying to communicate, so you can do it more clearly.

* * * * *

### RELATIONSHIP EXERCISE #1

Remember the PRACTICING NEUTRALITY exercise we did in chapter six? We took a thick pane of glass and put it between ourselves and someone who really bugged us. Then, keeping our emotional thermometers low, we discovered what they were trying to communicate to us, and what we wished to communicate to them, staying neutral during the process. For RELATIONSHIP EXERCISE #1, go back to that exercise and do it again,

153

this time with someone with whom you are in close relationship.

If you don't have anyone in your life in that category right now, imagine your ideal partner, and do the exercise with them. Or you can think back to a close relationship that occurred in the past, and do the exercise using that person.

Another helpful exercise for relationships is a slight modification of the Money Exercise we did above.

## RELATIONSHIP EXERCISE #2

*Sit down and make yourself comfortable. Close your eyes. Take a few deep breaths. While you are breathing, imagine that the air around you is filled with sparkling bits of golden energy. As you continue to breathe, breathe in the sparkling bits of golden energy.*

*This golden energy represents the life force, vitality, and wellness. This golden energy gently dissolves any tension, any discomfort, any distraction. Feel them release with every exhalation. Feel yourself inhaling the sparkling bits of golden energy, and let them refresh you. With every exhalation, let go of all your tension, discomfort and distractions.*

*Now direct the sparkling bits of golden energy to every part of you as you did in the health exercise. If you did not do the health exercise, just relax and breathe the sparkling bits of golden energy in deeply. Let the energy circulate through all parts of your body. Let your exhalations release all tensions, distractions and discomforts.*

*Take a few moments to think about relationships. Let an image form in your mind that represents your feelings about relationships. Take your time. There is no need to*

*force anything here. We all have feelings about relation-*
*ships, and the most appropriate image and symbol will*
*appear automatically.*

  *Place the image that symbolizes relationships to you*
*above the top of your head. Take a few moments to feel it*
*there. Does it have weight? Does it take up space? How*
*does it feel up there?*
  *Now, let a piece of this symbol break off and drop into*
*your body. Just open up and let the piece of this symbol*
*fall into you. It will land somewhere, there will be some-*
*place where the symbol lands and feels stuck or lodged.*
  *Perhaps it will lodge in more than one place. That is*
*fine. See if you can notice where it first lodged, or where it*
*seems heaviest. Now, let your awareness go to that place*
*where it is heaviest, or where the symbol is lodged. Take a*
*few moments to sense how it feels, how it would look if*
*you could see it, and what texture(s) and color(s) it has.*

*Ask the following questions and wait for an answer. If no answer occurs, just go on to the next question.*

*Are there any memories associated with this feeling?*

*If this feeling could talk, what would it say to me?*

*How does this feeling affect my attitude and feelings about relationships? Is it supportive? Does it interfere?*

*Think of a current situation which involves a particular relationship. How would this feeling approach and deal with this issue which is in my life right now?*

*If this feeling disappeared how would I approach this situation?*

*Say thank you for any and all of the information you have received. Release the feeling in your body and let the image above your head gently dissolve.*

*Feel yourself breathing deeply, and gently bring yourself back into your chair. When you are ready you can open your eyes. Record your experience in your journal.*

\* \* \* \* \*

This exercise can give even more insight into how our fears and desires support or interfere with our relationships. Your Intuition is a valuable tool in understanding relationships. Most of us can recognize that relationships are not usually rational. They are emotional and heartfelt. Our Intuition can guide us through the process of sorting out the emotions that lead to deeper intimacy and truthfulness from those that lead to frustration, loneliness and withdrawal.

One student did this exercise with his fiance. The symbol was their wedding ring. He felt it drop into his stomach. It gave him a feeling is nausea. Then his Intuition spoke to him. He realized that he had been avoiding helping out with the wedding plans and decisions. On further reflection, he realized how scared he was of getting married. After writing about his fears in his journal and expressing them to the class, and eventually to his fiance, he felt much better and could become involved with the plans. What happened to his fear?

It did not just disappear, but it became something he was aware of and could deal with. When he did not recognize his fear, he was controlled by it., without being consciously aware of that fact.

Another person did this exercise with his boss. He was having difficulty talking to him and wanted to explore why. The symbol for his boss dropped into his head. The intuitive impression that emerged was that he was not telling his boss what he really thought. He was so busy trying to figure out what his boss wanted to hear, that he was not sure himself of what he really wanted to say. Consequently, his communication was coming out all jumbled up. This realization helped him to sort out what we wanted to say, what he thought his boss wanted to hear, and improve his communication.

## Consistent Intuition Workout

With these tools, you can develop a deep and lasting relationship with your Intuition. It is now up to you to practice, workout, test, evaluate and utilize what you have learned. Intuition is infinitely patient. It won't go away. It will persist in giving you messages. You may not listen. You may misinterpret. Your fears may take advantage of you.

But keep working out with your Intuition. Your

Maintenance Program will keep your Intuition in top form, available and reliable whenever you need it.

## Intuition and Logic

Intuition is a valuable source of information. It is not meant to replace logical and rational thinking, but to enhance it. Allowing your intuitive impressions into your decision-making process will engage your whole self in whatever you decide to do. If you work against your Intuition, only part of you will be working. Make your Intuition your friend. Create a dialogue between the two of you. Listening to Intuition can make life an adventure to explore. Enjoy it!

# Suggested Reading

Intuitive Manager: Integrating Left and Right Brain Management Skills, *Weston H. Agor*. Prentice Hall, 1984.

The Tao of Psychology, *Jean Shinoda Bolen*. Harper & Row, 1979.

Creative Visualization, *Shakti Gawain*. Bantam, 1982.

The Intuitive Edge: Understanding Intuition & Applying It in Everyday Life, *Phillip Goldberg*. Tarcher, 1985.

Love is Letting Go of Fear, *Gerald Jampolsky*. Bantam, 1982.

The Intuitive Manager, *Roy Rowan*. Little, Brown & Co., 1986.

Zen Mind, Beginners Mind, *Shunryu Suzuki*. Weatherhill, 1970.

Awakening Intuition, *Frances Vaughn*. Doubleday, 1979.

The One Minute Manager, *Kenneth Blanchard & Spencer Johnson*. Berkley, 1986.

Focusing, *Eugene Gendlin*. Bantam, 1981.

Observing Self: Mysticism & Psychotherapy, *Arthur J. Deikman*. Beacon, 1983.

Right Brain Experience: An Intimate Program to Free the Powers of Your Imagination, *Marilee Zdenek*. McGraw-Hill, 1985.

## Intuition Workout (audio tape)

A dynamic audio presentation of highlights from the book. Read by the author, side one hits the essential parts of the text. Side two brings together the basic meditations, against a background of original music specially designed to induce a deep state of connection with your Intuition. The Intuition Workout tape is great as a gift, to listen to in the car, or as an accompaniment to the book: you can use the meditations from the tape as you read the book.

**90 minute tape, $9.95**

## Use Your Intuition

A 3 tape set containing six guided visualization exercises set to specially composed music. The exercises have been developed out of Nancy Rosanoff's years of experience in counselling people from all walks of life about getting in touch with their innermost feelings, and are a valuable aid in developing increased self-knowledge and self-mastery. Use Your Intuition is a much-expanded version of the basic Intuition Workout exercises. **3 tape set, $29.95**

## Introduction to the Chakras

A set of 3 audio tapes designed to open your awareness of the centers of vital energy within the human body. Set to original music, these meditations relax and soothe as they awaken your mind to your inherent potential. Some of the meditations are:
- Affirmations for the Chakras
- Information from the Chakras
- Self-guided Exploration of the Chakras    **3 tape set, $29.95**

## Order Form

| Title | Item | Price | Quan. | Total |
|---|---|---|---|---|
| **Intuition Workout** (book) | 13-7 | $9.95 | | |
| (tape) | 30-7 | $9.95 | | |
| **Use Your Intuition** (3 tape set) | 33-7 | $29.95 | | |
| **Intro. to the Chakras** (3 tape set) | 40-2 | $29.95 | | |
| SUBTOTAL | | | | |
| Calif. residents add 7% sales tax | | | | |
| Shipping: | | | | |
| (Book rate: $1.50 for first item, 50¢ ea add. item. First Class/UPS $3.50 for first item, $1 ea add.) | | | | |
| **TOTAL check or money order enclosed** | | | | |

Your Name: _____
Address: _____
_____
Phone: ( ____ ) _____

Mail to: Aslan Publishing
310 Blue Ridge Drive
Boulder Creek, CA 95006
(408) 338-7504